EQUESTRIAN
STYLE

EQUESTRIAN STYLE

HOME DESIGN, COUTURE, AND COLLECTIONS FROM THE ECLECTIC TO THE ELEGANT

VICKY MOON

PHOTOGRAPHS BY MONA BOTWICK

DESIGN BY DINA DELL'ARCIPRETE/dk DESIGN PARTNERS, NYC

CLARKSON POTTER/PUBLISHERS

NEW YORK

Copyright © 2008 by Vicky Moon

All rights reserved.
Published in the United States by Clarkson Potter/Publishers, an imprint of the Crown
Publishing Group, a division of Random House, Inc., New York.
www.crownpublishing.com
www.clarksonpotter.com

Clarkson N. Potter is a trademark and Potter and colophon are registered trademarks
of Random House, Inc.

Library of Congress Cataloging-in-Publication Data
Moon, Vicky.
   Equestrian style: home design, couture, and collections from the eclectic to the
elegant / Vicky Moon.
   1. Collectibles in interior decoration.   2. Horses—Collectibles.   3. Horsemanship—
Miscellanea.   I. Title.
NK2115.5.C58M66 2008
747—dc22   2007036708

ISBN 978-0-307-39468-2

Printed in China

10 9 8 7 6 5 4 3 2 1

First Edition

To Lenny, with much love and gratitude

Contents

Introduction

EQUESTRIAN STYLE BEGINS WITH A BASIC LOVE OF HORSES.

Our coast-to-coast tour of the distinctive equestrian lifestyle starts with an iconic well-worn brass door knocker shaped like a horse's head and continues with trophies displayed on mantels and portraits of favorite horses on walls. It broadens with images of foxes, horses, and hounds on pillows, fabric, wallpaper, and china, and even spreads into the wardrobe—a bracelet of snaffle bits, earrings shaped like stirrups, a tie adorned with jockey helmets or racing silks. It extends to needlepoint horse motifs on shoes and belts and to hood ornaments on cars. It gathers momentum with fixtures that do double duty in the house and the stable: a tack hook that functions as a pot rack in the kitchen, a pair of bookends made from old polo mallets.

Equestrian style is more than a feisty, wet Jack Russell terrier, a pair of Wellington boots, and a tweed jacket. It goes beyond hanging a hunting print on the dining room wall to actually leaping over stone walls on your favorite hunter. An unspoken equestrian philosophy surpasses wearing an Hermès scarf; it celebrates riding over jumps in an Hermès saddle. Equestrian style reaches its apex among people who not only love horses, but also practically live with them.

True equestrian fashion often contains a contradiction, as when a man in a worn, muddy pair of boots carries an ever-so-proper walking stick, or a rider wears white breeches when the chances are they will be dirty at the end of the competition.

Equestrian style can be found inside homes in the horse havens of Wellington and Ocala, Florida, and in the nearby temporary horse-show stables, where some even hire a landscape designer to personalize their space. The traveling show-jumping caravan also includes specialty shops that overflow with horse-related accessories for the home.

The look is not limited to the East Coast, to the miles of pristine fence lines and rolling green pastures often associated with horse country. In the center of the bustling entertainment universe of Los Angeles there are numerous homes and stables that reflect a love of horses, too. Equestrian style everywhere is defined by the art of the British sporting masters—George Stubbs, John F. Herring Sr., Benjamin Marshall, and Alfred Munnings—as well today's masters: Andre Pater, Liza Todd Tivey, and Dagmar Cosby.

Even the architecture of barns is significant, from the New York City livery stables of times gone by to the flawless fields and immaculate stables in the heart of the Kentucky bluegrass region. And who would ever think equestrian style could influence the manner in which one entertains? But consider the mint

< 8 >

julep or a cup of burgoo, both mandatory for attendees of the Kentucky Derby, the races in Keeneland, the hunt breakfast, and the lavish hunt ball, all steeped in tradition and laced with ambiance.

The late Marion duPont Scott embodied equestrian style almost from the moment she was born in 1894. "I can't remember a time I didn't like horses," she once said. Mrs. Scott grew up and spent her life at Montpelier, the Virginia estate once owned by President James Madison and his wife, Dolley. Paintings by the great British sporting artists hung on the walls amid architectural pieces from Ben Franklin and Thomas Jefferson, but her most cherished objects were the hundreds of black-and-white photos of her horses, including Battleship, a son of the great Man o' War and the first American-owned and -bred horse to capture England's Grand National Steeplechase, in 1938.

While some horse owners today might buy a potential racehorse and hope for the best, Mrs. Scott devoted herself to studying bloodlines and breeding a string of champion Thoroughbreds. She spent as much time in the barns and at the training track watching her horses prepare as did the people who were given the official task. And when she lost a beloved equine friend, she would bury the horse in the same hallowed grounds where the former president and his wife were laid to rest. For Mrs. Scott and others who epitomize equestrian style, horses and humans have equal rights. The adoration of a four-legged friend extends beyond the great moments of victory or long, exhilarating rides through the woods to memorializing the horse for eternity.

For this book, I visited horse lovers around the country who get up before the sun in order to make their horse's living spaces comfortable (and clean), who work for hours perfecting their performance in the ring, in the field, and at the track. This is a full-time commitment, the return for which is unconditional love and an unspoken bond. When the last bit of straw has been swept up, these horse owners trade their jeans and tweeds for ball gowns and scarlet jackets and dance at the hunt ball into the wee hours—and then start the routine all over again at the barn.

As you tour these homes, stables, and estates, you will see carriages, sparkling trophies, horse paintings galore, and Eclipse Awards (often displayed unceremoniously on a bookshelf). Equestrian style is an enduring tradition.

Part 1: In the Field

FOR TRAIPSING THROUGH THE

field at a steeplechase event in the hunt country, equestrian style mandates a pair of Wellingtons. First made of leather to the specifications of the Duke of Wellington in 1817, these distinctive boots were changed to the classic military green rubber in 1856. You never know when it might rain, so throw them in the back of the truck.

Ladies, while stomping divots at a high-goal polo match, only the most expensive pair of slingbacks will do. When yours are broken in and stained, you can proudly declare they were wrecked in Wellington, Florida, or at Cowdray Park in England. On a cross-country trick-or-treat jaunt on horseback, bring along your imagination and a few carrots for the ponies.

For the annual hunt ball, gentlemen are advised to wear scarlet, and ladies might want to don a pair of black velvet dancing slippers for a night of twirling on the dance floor. At an elegant holiday hunt breakfast, custom red-glazed walls shimmer, and spectacular equine sculptures mesmerize. Guests must always bid a hearty "good morning" to fellow riders and the gracious hosts.

Finally, when you are exhausted after all the sporting and social events, the National Sporting Library in Middleburg, Virginia, offers the perfect place to find some peace and quiet and read a great sporting book.

OPPOSITE, CLOCKWISE FROM TOP LEFT: A hand-painted sign at the Fenwick family's Maryland farm. Trainer Doug Fout exercises some of his steeplechase horses in Virginia. The New Bridge La Dolfina polo team celebrates in Florida. Bill and Elizabeth Wolf ride out for a day in the countryside. Charlie and Sherry Fenwick and Ollie share a moment in their country kitchen. *Elegant* is the word for the holiday mantel decoration of red silk amaryllis with sprigs of live evergreen at Somerset Farm. Caroline Fout gets ready to ride. CENTER: Charlie Fenwick was uninjured in this dramatic dismount off Happy Orphan in the 1974 Maryland Hunt Cup.

THE SPORT OF QUEENS

The line formed . . . and rebroke. Waves of the sea. Drawing a breath . . . breaking. Velvet fifth from the rail, between a bay and a brown. The Starter had long finished his instructions. Nothing more was said aloud, but low oaths flew, the cursing and grumbling flashed like a storm.

—Enid Bagnold, *National Velvet* (1935)

Sherry Fenwick has a keen sense of color, a gift for choosing just the right fabric, and an eye for detail. She blends these talents with a passion for horses in the country home she shares with her husband, Charles Fenwick Jr., in Baltimore County, Maryland.

Known as Worthington Valley, the region is rich in horse history. The broader landscape embraces the Elkridge-Harford Hunt, the Green Spring Valley Hunt, My Lady's Manor, and the Howard County–Iron Bridge Hounds.

Sherry began with a blank canvas when she and Charlie were married in 1996. The house he built in 1984 on 140 acres was not yet decorated. The arched dormers breaking the eave line and a concave cat-slide roof on the entrance portico reveal a French influence.

Sherry had a treasure trove of Fenwick heirlooms to launch her decorating project, including numerous cherished trophies Charlie won riding in steeplechase races around the world, among them the Maryland Hunt Cup; the 1980 Grand National Steeplechase in Aintree, England; and the American Grand National, part of which is run over their property, and which Charlie has won a record ten times.

Sherry's panache greets visitors in the front hall, which hints at the character of the house. The brick floor is set in a herringbone pattern and sealed with a high-gloss lacquer that resists damage from boots in this heavily trodden foyer. A nineteenth-century French Transition–style commode with a black marble top displays the 1987 Eclipse Award Charlie won as trainer of Dogwood Stables' champion steeplechase horse Inlander. The Delft blue wallpaper accents an antique English flow-blue platter made with cobalt glaze, inspired by Asian designs, and a tall silver Maryland Hunt Cup tankard (won by Charlie, of course). The Heriz Persian rug in muted red and pink tones with a touch of blue is an apt complement.

Odie and Hammer, a frisky pair of Jack Russell terriers, keep their owners company. They also appear in the entry hall painting of steeplechase champion Talkin Butter along with the Fenwicks' dogs Pepper, an English cocker, and Ethel, a Labrador retriever. The Fenwicks commissioned artist Larry Wheeler to do the painting in 1999.

A long Brighton bench with a rush seat of bamboo that dates to 1820 serves as a place for guests to leave their bags. "With this eclectic mix of furniture and accessories, a bit eccentric is the way I would describe how our home is decorated," Sherry says. "I have no formula or organizing principle."

Throughout the house, Sherry's ability to blend old, new, formal, and fun is enviable. The brick floor extends from the entryway into the dining room. In an otherwise serious and formal room, she has placed a tall piece of contemporary folk art, a spirit keeper titled *Great Delight,* which she purchased at the Laguna Beach Art Festival.

< 15 >

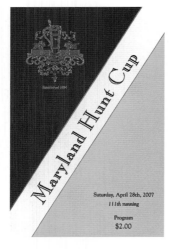

Maryland Hunt Cup

Saturday, April 28th, 2007
111th running

Program
$2.00

In the dining room, the central piece of art is a painting of a steeplechase horse called Billy Barton by British artist Thomas Earl (1864–1943). The horse, owned by Charlie's grandfather Howard Bruce, inspired Charlie to devote his life to winning the Grand National in England. The Grand National Steeplechase was first run in 1839 and won by the appropriately named Lottery. It was the first steeplechase to offer big money to the winner. Today, the purse is £700,000, more than $1.4 million.

The race takes place in early spring in Aintree, England, a small town near Liverpool also known for its marmalade. It is run over four and a half miles with thirty towering, intimidating, and ominous obstacles such as the famous Becher's Brook, named in honor of Captain William Becher, who fell here in 1939 and huddled in the water on the far side until the field had passed.

Billy Barton was one jump away from glory in the legendary steeplechase in 1928 when jockey Tommy Cullinan was tossed. He remounted, and Billy Barton finished second to Tipperary Tim, the only other horse to finish that year. The next year, Billy Barton returned and was featured on the cover of *Time* magazine on March 18, 1929. He finished out of the money.

Charlie had a lifetime to look at the painting of Billy Barton and to reflect on the Grand National, which was a favorite subject of Earl's. A second painting by Earl of Billy Barton and Whistler, a favorite hunter of Charlie's grandmother Mary Graham Bruce, also hangs in the dining room.

Charlie first entered the English Grand National in 1979 and was brought down at the Chair, a 5-foot-high, 5-foot-wide monstrosity that also includes a 3-foot ditch. He returned the next year and won the legendary race on Ben Nevis II at odds of 40 to 1. Charlie and Ben Nevis II also earned the distinction of being only the second American entry in 137 years to win.

"Horses, steeplechase horses in particular, are almost like an addiction," says Charlie, who rides each morning and then heads back to the house to change for his job running a luxury car dealership.

"The house has to function for hardworking horse trainers, as both Charlie and Sherry are very involved with the stables on the property," says architect Ann Hagerty, whose firm did several renovations on the home. "Over the years, the house has become more open to improve entertaining, to work more intimately for the Fenwicks, and also to relate more to the open rolling fields surrounding the house."

In the great room across the back of the house, two distinct styles mingle perfectly. At one end of the room, a formal seating area is wrapped in French country Pierre Deux Île de France yellow-and-blue wallpaper. "The den was opened to the lowered living room with a simple pair of flanking columns in a trimmed opening," says Ann. She designed the valance and window treatments using Robert Allen's Hermès pattern in goldenrod.

A soft-toned yellow sofa covered in a cotton moiré seats five people comfortably. The sofa is anchored by a wing chair upholstered with a Jane Churchill velvet in a color called Sunshine from Cowtan & Tout; an 8-inch wool bullion fringe adds kick. A companion wing chair in a flaxen print completes the seating area.

Bookshelves flank the fireplace, filled with books, more trophies, and additional pieces of flow blue. Sherry purchased the whimsical fireplace screen while antique

PREVIOUS PAGES, LEFT: Sherry Fenwick pauses on a circa 1820 Brighton bench in the front hall with Ollie, Odie, and Hammer. The Delft blue wallpaper in the foyer is from Lee Jofa in the Solomon's Seal pattern and is carried through in the dining room. OPPOSITE, CLOCKWISE FROM TOP LEFT: A large pergola on the south side of the house protects the den from extreme summer sun and creates a defined area for entertaining. Billy Barton was featured on the March 18, 1929, cover of *Time* magazine. There is no decorating detail overlooked by Sherry Fenwick, right down to the coordinating welting on the dining room chair cushions. Dagmar Cosby's whimsical primitive painting holds a place of honor. Charlie and Ben Nevis II won the English Grand National Steeplechase in 1980. FOLLOWING PAGES: The Fenwicks' great room combines the formal and the casual.

TIME

The Weekly Newsmagazine

BILLY BARTON

Volume XIII Number 11

hunting in Virginia. A small collection of yellow earthenware plates with black transfer adorns the mantel alongside a porcelain figurine of a mare and foal made by the British firm Beswick. The painting over the mantel, *Hounds,* by B. A. Hyland (signed and dated 1883), hints at another favorite Fenwick pastime, foxhunting.

On the opposite end of the great room, walls covered with old cedar barn siding create a cozy atmosphere. Silk taffeta curtains in a color Sherry describes as "celery" dress up the French doors. Edged with tasseled fringe, they were made to puddle gently on the floor.

Above the fireplace, which is finished in fieldstone, an antique barn beam serving as a mantel holds family photos and the silver Brooklawn Challenge Cup, first presented in 1929 and won by Charlie in 1983. Over the mantel a brass-and-copper wall sculpture of foxes by Kirk McMinn is another reference to foxhunting.

Everywhere, Sherry has gathered masses of pillows featuring dogs and horses in needlepoint and prints, all lavishly trimmed and edged with tassels and braid. A George III mahogany cylinder desk from the late eighteenth century holds more photos and an oversize silver two-handled trophy won by none other than Billy Barton in the 1927 New Jersey Hunt Cup. Talkin Butter, the Fenwicks' horse featured in the front hall painting, won the same race in 1998.

A primitive painting in bright colors by another favorite artist, Dagmar Cosby of Oakton, Virginia, hangs over the desk. "It's called *A Day in the Country* and is a two-by-three-foot interpretation of the Maryland Hunt Cup and the Grand National combined," Sherry explains.

Dagmar is a frequent guest at the Fenwicks'. "The Fenwicks love to entertain, and they open their house to many local and international friends," says Ann, who kept this in mind while doing the architectural renovations.

In the spring of 2005, the Fenwicks invited British mystery writer Dick Francis to come for a weekend of races. Before he was a writer, Dick was a jockey. He was within 40 yards of glory at the English Grand National in 1956 when Devon Loch, a jumper owned by Queen Elizabeth the Queen Mother, inexplicably fell. The film clip is usually part of the annual television coverage of the race.

In 1957, Dick retired from racing following a serious fall. He wrote his autobiography, *The Sport of Queens,* which led to a job covering racing for the London *Sunday Express.* In 1962, his first thriller, *Dead Cert,* was published. Since then, he has written forty mysteries, several of which have been on the *New York Times* bestseller list. All of them are set against a backdrop of horses and the world of racing.

When the Fenwicks introduced Dick and Dagmar, a romance followed. Since then, Dagmar, sixtyish, and Dick, eightyish, meet whenever possible, at one of his book signings in New York, or at one of her art shows in Virginia. In between, they carry on as do many others—with daily notes by e-mail.

Riding for the royal family, Dick has met Queen Elizabeth II many times. And in 2007, Sherry and Charlie also met the queen, whose love of horses is well documented, at a British Embassy garden party in Washington. They were among the guests who received a coveted gold-engraved invitation.

There was never a question of what Sherry would wear for the royal introduction. The Swiss cotton suit she had made in a butter color was inspired by an old Chanel suit purchased at the Hopkins Best-Dressed Sale, a charity of which Sherry has served as cochair. Her knack for putting together colors and fabrics is clearly not limited to interiors.

OPPOSITE, CLOCKWISE FROM TOP LEFT: One end of the great room has a formal French influence. The stationary Equicizer horse in the dressing room was invented by Eclipse Award–winning jockey Frank Lovato Jr. to aid in his own recovery from a racing accident. The mantel has accent pieces of yellow earthenware plates with black transfer and a porcelain mare and foal figurine from the British firm Beswick. Charlie's cobalt blue English Grand National Trophy was made by Aynsley China. Speaking of her eclectic pairing of textiles and furnishings, as in this corner of the great room, Sherry says, "I feel blessed to have a very distinctive taste."

CHAMPAGNE AND CHUKKERS

Now a polo-pony is like a poet. If he is born with a love for the game, he can be made. The Maltese Cat knew that bamboos grew solely in order that polo-balls might be turned from their roots, that grain was given to ponies to keep them in hard condition, and that ponies were shod to prevent them slipping on a turn. But, besides all these things, he knew every trick and device of the finest game of the world, and for two seasons he had been teaching the others all he knew or guessed.

—Rudyard Kipling, *The Maltese Cat* (1894)

The ancient, aristocratic, and extravagant sport of polo was clearly an inspiration for fashion designer Ralph Lauren when he launched his Polo line in 1968. He brought the tweed hacking jacket to the mainstream, and the equestrian style endures. When the Polo Black line of men's fragrance was introduced in 2005, the handsome Argentinian Ignacio "Nacho" Figueras became the model gazing out from glossy magazines worldwide.

But Nacho is not just another pretty face. His day job is playing polo for the Black Watch polo team. This in turn has spawned Ralph Lauren's Black Watch line of clothing: traditional shirts worn by the players and a dressy line of spectator outfits—linen trousers and blazers for men and flowing floral dresses for women to wear while sipping a flute of champagne. However, Nacho is not the only professional polo player to enter the world of fashion.

AVENUE ALVEAR

At number 1315 on the fashionable Avenue Alvear in bustling Buenos Aires is a shop called La Dolfina. Inside are life-size photos of the owner, Adolfo Cambiaso, one of Argentina's most famous sportsmen. He does not play soccer, Argentina's national pastime, but some will tell you he can dribble the ball as well as the legendary Maradona.

Thirty-something "Adolfito" Cambiaso is the number one polo player in the world. He is Tiger Woods with a polo mallet and Roger Federer on a horse, all wrapped into one lithe and lanky body. In 1993, at age seventeen, he was the youngest player in history to achieve a ten-goal rating, the sport's highest accolade, awarded by the United States Polo Association and based on scoring history and prowess. He's ridden on the winning team in the U.S. Open, the Argentine Open, and the Queen's Cup on multiple occasions.

On the field, Cambiaso brings together daring instinct and authoritarian execution. He earns several million dollars a year riding and even more selling polo ponies whose price tags are often in the six figures.

Cambiaso keeps more than six hundred ponies on his estate, La Dolfina, outside of Buenos Aires, and at a larger ranch in Córdoba. He flies around the world to play polo in Florida, Spain, Dubai, and Great Britain. It was once reported that the polo-playing English prince Harry sought Cambiaso as his personal coach.

Cambiaso's line of clothing includes jeans, blazers, and,

of course, polo shirts, boots, and luggage. It also includes his signature La Dolfina jersey, which polo fans don like football fans wear football jerseys in the United States. He has two shops in Buenos Aires, one in the Galerías Pacifico and the other in the posh section called Recoleta. There is another in La Plata, Argentina, and one in Chile, with plans for branches in the United States.

Cambiaso prepares for a game by getting into one of his La Dolfina jerseys. He pulls on his boots and straps on knee pads. He discusses strategy with teammates as they gather under a small tent at the end of the field. Spectators in the grandstands settle into their seats and perhaps grab a drink at the bar.

A polo match consists of six chukkers, or playing periods, of seven minutes each. As part of the tradition of the sport, spectators are urged to walk on the field to stomp down the divots at halftime. During the winter season at the International Polo Club Palm Beach, complimentary flutes of Roederer Estate Anderson Valley brut champagne are served at midfield.

Cambiaso mesmerizes the crowd. At the end of the match, he peels off his sweaty La Dolfina shirt. The women swoon as he puts on a new one; polo players are notoriously immodest. As he approaches the trophy table, the corks fly again, and Cambiaso celebrates yet another victory.

PREVIOUS PAGES, RIGHT: The Cartier International Polo Tournament takes place each July at the Guards Polo Club in England. OPPOSITE: Nine-goaler Matías Magrini of Argentina. LEFT, FROM TOP: A young polo player wears the shirt of his favorite player. Knee pads are essential. Cambiaso chases down an opponent. FOLLOWING PAGES: According to Winston Churchill, "A polo handicap is your passport to the world."

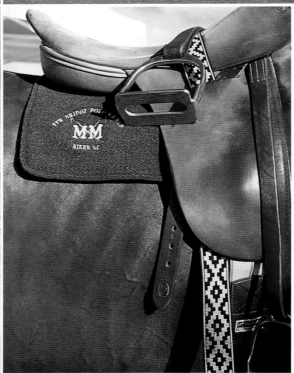

Cartier

Mirella Levinas   Fariba Jahanbani

together with

Mr. and Mrs. Tareq Salahi   Mr. Charles A. Muldoon
Co-Chairs, America's Cup   Director of Polo, America's Cup

request the pleasure of your company for
a cocktail reception to celebrate the

America's Cup of Polo

Thursday, April 26
six until eight o'clock

Cartier
5471B Wisconsin Avenue
Chevy Chase

RUSS MCCALL

During the winter polo season, Cambiaso plays at the International Polo Club Palm Beach in Wellington, Florida, with Russ McCall's team, New Bridge. They call the team New Bridge La Dolfina by adding Cambiaso's stable and business name. As the patron (pronounced as if Spanish, "paa-trone") of the team, Russ finances it. (The weekly rates for players like Cambiaso are said to reach to $150,000.)

High finance such as this never occurred to Russ when he was growing up on Long Island during the

1950s. He remembers seeing photos of his grandfather, great-grandfather, and great-uncle playing polo at the Brooklyn Riding and Driving Club near Prospect Park. He dreamed of playing polo, and filed the dream away for the future.

As a young boy, Russ sold eggs door-to-door. While still in college he opened a wine and cheese shop, which grew into a chain of six shops that he later sold. From there he started Atlanta Foods International, a wholesale specialty and gourmet food distribution business in thirty-three states.

Forty years later, Russ retired and took up polo. He also stays involved in the wine business with the McCall Family Vineyard, producing pinot noir and red burgundy with 20 acres of vines on Long Island.

Russ and Matías Magrini, a nine-goal player from Argentina, are partners in the 800-acre New Bridge Polo and Country Club gated community in the horsey enclave of Aiken, South Carolina. There are polo fields, polo barns, polo matches, and polo ponies for sale. "This is my second childhood," Russ says.

> Johnny Lynn developed designs to accommodate the players. Most of his designs have the practicality of the sport in mind but can translate to street wear. The Windbreakers have slightly shorter fronts and are longer in the back than a jacket cut normally. "

BURLINGTON ARCADE

During the summer polo season, spectators and polo players celebrate with distinctive orange-label Veuve Clicquot champagne during the Gold Cup tournament at Cowdray Park Polo Club near Midhurst in West Sussex, England. On the trophy table are shirts from the British line Polistas, a term used in Argentina for polo players, designed by player Johnny Lynn. A Canadian, Johnny trained with his country's ski team, and after college landed in London to work in finance. He took up polo at the age of thirty-four and started promoting polo matches and putting team logos on caps and shirts.

Johnny was determined to expand his line. He even took his pitch to the British television series *Dragons' Den,* in which entrepreneurs pitch their product in order to win financial backing. He didn't win, but Johnny's resolve materialized in 2001, and he now has a retail boutique in the upscale Burlington Arcade in the Mayfair section of London, near Bond Street.

LEFT, FROM TOP: Johnny Lynn's line of polo-inspired clothing can be found in the fashionable Burlington Arcade in London. The Veuve Clicquot Gold Cup tournament takes place during the summer season at Cowdray Park near Midhurst in West Sussex, England. The area is often referred to as the home of British Polo.

"The standard polo shirts, baseball caps, and fleeces found in this sector were, in my opinion, not up to scratch for top brands and luxury goods companies trying to associate themselves with the 'king of sports,'" Johnny says. He developed designs to accommodate the players. Most of Johnny's designs have the practicality of the sport in mind but can translate to street wear. The Windbreakers have slightly shorter fronts and are longer in the back than a jacket cut normally. "This is so there isn't too much material in the front to bulge when a player bends over to hit a polo ball and so that his or her backside isn't exposed while in that position," Johnny notes. "Moreover, arms are slightly longer so the cuffs don't creep up your forearms when you put your rein hand forward or swing your mallet."

Johnny's Polistas line also includes ties, blazers, socks, and chino shorts. "In fact, our philosophy has been to design everything one might need for a two-week trip to play polo in an exotic location, including the luggage to put it all in," he says. And although he does not yet have the coveted Royal Warrant, bestowed as an indication of royal retail approval, the polo-playing princes William and Harry started appearing frequently in the press wearing Polistas gear they had won during a polo match. "This proved that our garments had indeed become their old favorites," Johnny adds.

RIGHT, FROM TOP: Early-morning exercise sessions for polo ponies are streamlined by taking four or more ponies for a jog. Upon close inspection, the understated English tailgate includes several bottles of bubbles. Stomping the divots on the polo pitch takes place at halftime.

NANO

In the United States, the authentic polo look can be found at La Martina and Polo Gear in Wellington, Florida. This is where the real polo players come to buy attire, equipment, and a colorful array of jerseys from the French, Canadian, and Australian teams; the jerseys easily translate into everyday clothing.

It is here that one will find the Argentinian former polo player Adriano "Nano" Perez in a cluttered workroom.

Just as Antonio Stradivari of Italy carefully crafted spruce, willow, and maple into masterpiece violins perfect in pitch and tone, Nano spends hours working with manau and batu, both types of cane from the palm family, and wood known as tipa, to produce exquisite custom-made polo mallets.

The cane comes from the jungles of Indonesia and Malaysia, with the precise location Nano's trade secret. The tipa (botanical name *Tipuana tipu*) is available only in northern Argentina and parts of Brazil and Paraguay.

Aged between fifteen and thirty years, the mature canes are green when cut at the root and then trimmed to 9 feet long. They are boiled in palm oil for ten to fifteen minutes, emerging with a black covering. They are then washed in sand and water, which removes the black coating to reveal a golden hue, and dried and bundled for transport. Nano inspects each shipment, which must be sent to his Florida workshop with the proper importation papers. Nano then heats them over a fire to straighten them, and places them in a curing oven.

An ideal mallet has a cane and a head of equal weight. The cigar-shaped heads are made of the tough, close-grained tipa wood. They come in five shapes: oval—cut on each end in order to lift the ball; skene—with a flat bottom for more loft; standard—with smooth edges for more striking surface; oversize—following the same principle as a large tennis racket; and oversize/shaved—with a heavy,

dense head that is shaved at the bottom and retains its shape after many hits.

The overall weight of each mallet ranges from 15.87 ounces to more than 20 ounces, depending on the player's preference, which is often based on his or her height and strength. The length of the mallet, from 48 to 55 inches, is directly related to the size of the pony. Nano individualizes each grip, and the final step is usually choosing the colors to be painted on the heads.

Nano paints each mallet with the player's colors. Actor and polo aficionado Tommy Lee Jones has an upside-down 7 logo for his San Saba team on the head of his mallets, with the tips painted in red. Adolfo Cambiaso has his mallet tips finished in white. Some players have patterns such as the British flag or the flag of Texas painted on the heads.

Nano's wife, Irene Perez, assists in personalizing each mallet with the player's initials and then finishes it off with Nano's logo of a pair of crossed mallets on the head and just below the handle. Each mallet costs about $120; professional players order ten to twenty at a time for each season in Wellington, England, and Argentina.

Almost everyone who plays polo attributes success to a good pony, a mount that can gallop with the wind, then turn on a dime and leave nine cents' change. Many players say the pony accounts for 70 to 80 percent of the equation.

Assuming each player has a superior string of six to twelve high-powered ponies, the next concern is equipment. Players gallop at thirty to forty miles per hour toward the ball, and as they swing their sticks, accuracy and execution are crucial. An artist like Stradivari, Nano found his niche in creating a different type of instrument—one that nevertheless plays sweet music when the thud of wood against ball signals the perfectly struck shot.

SCARLET IF CONVENIENT

In the annals of sport in America there has been no family which for parts of three centuries has been longer and more honorably connected with foxhunting than the Dulanys.

—Harry Worcester Smith, sportsman and founder of the Masters of Foxhounds Association (1941)

As master of foxhounds and huntsman of the Carrollton Hounds, Dulany Jones Noble carries on the Dulany family's equestrian pursuits in a graceful and effortless manner. As master, she is entitled to wear the vivid scarlet jacket, which provides visibility and is a coveted indication of accomplishment. The vibrant color has evolved into an emblematic equestrian icon.

Dulany begins her day in the horse country of Carroll County, northwest of Baltimore, exercising her big bay Thoroughbred, Custer Road. She then travels fifteen minutes to the hunt kennels to check on the hounds. On Wednesdays and Sundays, she leads fields of up to fifty faithful foxhunters on a chase through the countryside.

Dulany's devotion to horses began with Cream Puff, an aptly named Welsh pony. "I was about two years old," she recalls. Her mother, Maud Dulany Barker Jones, an expert horsewoman, taught her to ride. Her mother also rode with the Carrollton Hounds, and the original engraved invitations she received to join the hunt in the early 1940s are part of the family memorabilia. (There are also invitations to the Bachelor's Cotillion and the Baltimore Assembly, long-standing social events.)

To this day, one must be invited to join the Carrollton Hounds, founded by Harry Straus, who owned the American Totalisator Company of Baltimore, which calculated pari-mutuel odds at racetracks around the country.

"We're an unrecognized foxhunting club," Dulany says, noting that they are not part of the governing body of the Masters of Foxhounds Association of America, which oversees 170 member hunts. "We adhere to all the customs of traditional foxhunting as practiced by other recognized clubs. We're just a very small, local, and all-volunteer organization."

The official foxhunting season runs from November to March. A fixture card is sent to notify members where to gather. The names of the farms—George Brooks-Lippy's Silos, High Hay Fields, Ship's Quarters, Terra Rubra—are entertaining to read.

When not dealing with horses and hounds, Dulany has a full-time day job as the owner of Gala Cloths by Dulany. Her staff of eighteen employees rents tablecloths for special occasions: conventions, weddings, and receptions. These are not just any old tablecloths. Each is designed by Dulany from fabric she finds and is made by a team of talented sewers. "I have more than three hundred designs and patterns and the depth to do one design for up to one thousand people," she says.

Gala Cloths by Dulany also maintains an inventory of luncheon, dinner, and buffet napkins, chair covers, and other accessories. The coordinating patterns feature a bunch of grapes matched with grapevines, toile, or classic cabbage-rose chintz with overlays of checks or stripes. On

<33>

any given weekend, Dulany's business furnishes cloths for thirty to forty events. In one year, her business provided table coverings for 2,700 parties.

Of course, Dulany's linens adorned the tables for the Carrollton Hounds Hunt Ball. Dulany herself coordinated and styled the event, which was held to celebrate sixty years of the hunt.

"I was a theater major in college and have always loved doing any type of production," she says. The ball took place at the majestic Garrett-Jacobs Mansion on Mount Vernon Square in downtown Baltimore. The Italian Renaissance–style rose-colored sandstone building encompasses four grand town houses and dates to 1853; architects Stanford White and John Russell Pope were involved in various stages of development and renovations.

Now, as the private Engineering Society of Baltimore, the structure encompasses forty rooms with sixteen fireplaces and one hundred windows, some of which are Tiffany.

A long table in the drawing room was covered with silent auction items, such as "Unbridled Love," a basket of items to spoil your horse with, including an Amish-made leather bridle and breastplate; "Hold Your Horses," with rubber reins and leather riding gloves; and "Lady in Red," a scarlet wool jacket with a horse motif.

The Carrollton Hounds newsletter encouraged women to wear long dresses and ball gowns for the black-tie party. "Show all the skin you dare, and wear as much bling as you can. Color is important." Dulany wore a long black satin skirt and a scarlet sequined top adorned with an antique diamond crescent-moon pin inherited from her mother.

Color was also significant for the men. The invitation discreetly advised, "Scarlet if convenient." Male members of the hunt, who have earned the privilege, were invited to wear a formal scarlet tailcoat.

Following drinks and bidding on the silent auction items, guests moved into the ballroom. Floor-length hunter-green damask tablecloths accented Spode china featuring foxhunting scenes designed by the well-known British sporting artist John Frederick Herring Sr.

Josiah Spode founded the Spode Pottery Company in Stoke-on-Trent, England, in 1767, and Spode is the oldest pottery company still operating on its original site.

When William Taylor Copeland, an alderman and lord mayor of London, took over Spode in 1947, he provided Herring with a cottage on his estate in Essex. In exchange for rent, Herring painted pictures of racehorses and hunting life.

Known as "The Hunt," the collection was manufactured between 1930 and the mid-1990s. Each earthenware plate has a different foxhunting scene by Herring; a decoration in the middle of each plate resembles a hand-colored hunting print, and a green band surrounds it. Titles appear on the bottom of each plate: "Full Cry," "Throwing Off," "The Find," "Taking the Lead," and "First Over." Close examination of the plates reveals that some of the riders are wearing scarlet jackets.

PREVIOUS PAGES, LEFT: The scarlet hunting and formal evening jackets are sporadically called pink coats, which refers to an unconfirmed legend that the attire was first made by a British tailor by the name of Pink or Pinque. ABOVE: A 1942 invitation to Maud Dulany Barker Jones to join the Carrollton Hounds, and a vintage photo of Maud out riding. OPPOSITE: Dulany Jones Noble (top and bottom right) leads the Carrollton Hounds at the hunt ball and in the hunt field. Her green taffeta tablecloths (below left) were used to complement the Spode hunting plates.

The Carrollton Hounds
Double Anniversary Celebration

2006
Hunt Ball

1936-1949

1976-2006

Friday, October 27, 2006
7:30 P.M.

at the Engineers Club
Garrett-Jacobs Mansion

WELL READ

There are sports—football, baseball, and basketball—and then there is sport: foxhunting, shooting clays, and angling. The essence of the noble and traditional life of sport can be found on the walls and shelves at the National Sporting Library in Middleburg, Virginia.

Founded in 1954, the library was designed to subtly echo the indigenous vernacular of this breathtaking corner of the countryside. Local architect and foxhunter Tommy Beach incorporated fieldstone, a metal roof, stucco, and wood siding. The building is best defined as a dignified Virginia farmhouse with a Federal flair. Beach conceived ways to brand the structures as old. For example, he dictated that the stone be purposely set irregularly, and the stucco was finished with imperfect corners and then whitewashed.

The library contains 16,000 volumes, including rare books on equitation theory and horse care such as *Méthode et invention nouvelle de dresser les chevaux* (1657), by the Duke of Newcastle, and *École de cavalerie* (1733), by François Robichon de La Guérinière, as well as the 205-volume collection of German riding master Ludwig Hunersdorf (1748–1812).

Noted for its permanent collection of art, the library holds work by sporting artists Edward Troye, John Emms, Alfred de Dreux, John Frederick Herring Sr., and Henry Alken. In addition, the library hosts lectures and presentations, such as a book signing by Paul Cronin, who wrote *Schooling and Riding the Sport Horse*.

Visitors from around the world come to the serene alcoves of the library, perhaps to translate an early sixteenth-century Italian book on dressage, research the evolution of bit design, or add to a draft on the famous Palio horse race through the streets of Siena, Italy.

To bibliophiles who want to begin an equestrian-based library of their own, Rick Stoutamyer of Undercover Books in Marshall, Virginia, says, "Equestrian-related collections could be built around coaching, polo, foxhunting, Thoroughbred racing, steeplechase racing, three-day eventing, show jumping, or architecture related to barns, stables, and kennels."

Rick recommends the bibliography of the Paul Mellon collection, *Books on the Horse and Horsemanship: Riding, Hunting, Breeding, and Racing, 1400–1941,* by John Podeschi. "It's useful for its chronological organization showing the development of equestrian books and manuscripts over a five-hundred-year span and for its reproductions of some of the original illustrations within the books.

"Once you've decided what areas of interest you're going to pursue, you should become knowledgeable about the books that are available in those specific fields," Rick says. "The National Sporting Library book collection may be searched for free online. Begin searching using keywords such as *bibliography, polo, coaching,* et cetera."

He also lists *Horsemanship: A Bibliography of Printed Materials from the Sixteenth Century through 1974,* by Ellen Wells; *The Derrydale Press: A Bibliography,* by Colonel

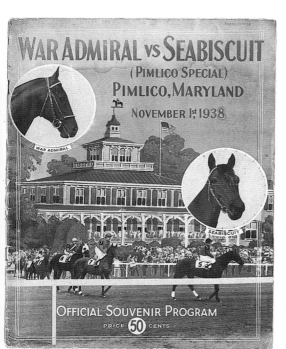

The Volte renverfee to the left.

WAR ADMIRAL vs SEABISCUIT
(PIMLICO SPECIAL)
PIMLICO, MARYLAND
NOVEMBER 1st, 1938

WAR ADMIRAL

SEABISCUIT

OFFICIAL SOUVENIR PROGRAM
PRICE 50 CENTS

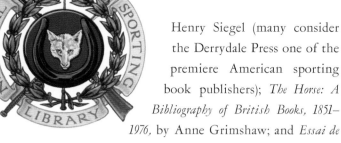

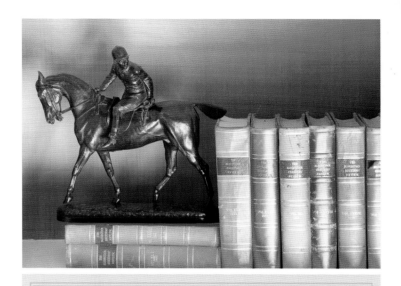

Henry Siegel (many consider the Derrydale Press one of the premiere American sporting book publishers); *The Horse: A Bibliography of British Books, 1851–1976,* by Anne Grimshaw; and *Essai de bibliographie hippique,* by Mennessier de la Lance. "This is useful for pre-twentieth-century French-language equestrian titles," he says.

In order to define your personal library, Rick says, "you'll need to go beyond just learning what titles are available in your field. Your next step is to learn why two copies of apparently the same exact title may have radically different prices separated by hundreds or thousands of dollars."

Condition, scarcity, and desirability all influence the monetary value of a book. "Older is not always better," Rick relates. "Many books printed four to five hundred years ago can be bought much more cheaply than some books printed during the twentieth century." And, he adds, the first edition of a book is not always the most valuable. "A later edition with hand-colored illustrations or illustrations by a famous artist may be more collectible."

The dust jacket can also be a factor in value. "A ten-thousand-dollar book in jacket might cost a thousand dollars without the jacket." He suggests buying a book in the best condition at the price you can afford.

Rick concludes, "A rare or scarce book is not necessarily a valuable book. It can be a first edition in great condition, and very few copies may exist, but if nobody wants it, it's not desirable."

OPPOSITE: In addition to holding a vast collection of manuscripts and rare books, the National Sporting Library hosts art exhibitions and lectures. OPPOSITE, CENTER RIGHT: The sculpture of a civil war horse by Tessa Pullen was commissioned by Paul Mellon. Sporting artists such as Frank Voss, Henry Alken, George Stubbs, and J. F. Herring Sr. are also represented.

CARING FOR YOUR BOOKS

Richard Hooper
Hooper's Books and Art, Washington, D.C.

Direct sunlight causes the most damage to books. A library with a large bank of windows, especially with a southern exposure, is a problem. Sunlight fades colors and dries out bindings. Today, however, special filtering glass for windows can be found. Neon lighting can also cause fading, and heat from radiators can cause drying. High humidity can foster mildew and mold.

Generally, if you're comfortable with the air-conditioning or heating temperatures in your house, your books probably are as well. Avoid hooking your fingertip behind the top of the spine when taking books from shelves; it tears that part of the book. It is best to slightly push in both books that sit next to the book you want and then grip the sides of the book you want to remove. Or, with your index finger, reach past the spine to the front of the book and tilt it out.

For the shelves, it doesn't matter whether you choose wood or steel. However, since a library is a matter of pleasure on a number of levels, one of them being aesthetic, the nicer the arrangement, the more one enjoys it.

Books are quite happy either upright or flat. Very large books are probably happier flat to relieve the stress that the weight of the pages can put on the spine. However, as a stack of books grows taller, it can become a bother to retrieve the one on the bottom.

TOP: *At the Start,* a watercolor by the French artist Alfred de Dreux (1810–1860). **ABOVE**: An eight-paneled screen signed as "invented by Thos Butler & executed at his house, Pall-Mall, London 1755" depicts eighteenth-century horses. **OPPOSITE**: Erick Haupt's oil on canvas of George Ohrstrom Sr., a founder of the library.

TRICK OR TREAT

The four members of the Fout family spend quite a bit of time puttering in the barn, working on the farm, and riding ponies in the fields at their home near The Plains, Virginia.

The days begin at five in the morning, when Doug Fout makes race entries for his horses on the computer and checks e-mail, departing for his Coosaw Stables by six. Doug is one of the top steeplechase trainers in the country. He trained Hirapour, a strapping Irish-bred horse owned by Ken and Maureen Luke of Atlanta, the 2004 Eclipse Horse of the Year Champion, with lifetime earnings of $658,000. He has sixty horses in training, half of which race on the flat at tracks up and down the East Coast. The jumpers, as steeplechase horses are called, compete in races in Saratoga Springs, New York; Fair Hill, Maryland; and Middleburg, Virginia, among other locales.

Beth Fout runs a small business training hunters, gallops racehorses for her husband, and keeps twins Caroline and Dunn's ponies in shape. All of this translates to plenty of mud and muck traipsed in and out of their white stucco farmhouse every day. So when the Fouts decided to renovate their kitchen and add more room to the house, the first item on the list was a mudroom.

The origin of the mudroom is utilitarian. Many old country homes had a small entryway for farmers to take off muddy boots and even overalls. Shedding shoes at the back door helps control dirt, mold, and bacteria.

The mudroom was never intended to be a fancy place, just a stopping-off point. These useful rooms have even crept into city architecture. According to the *Washington Post,* "The humble mudroom is a key feature sought by new-home buyers and remodelers." No longer just a space for storing boots, the mudroom now serves as a place to work on craft projects or gardening or do laundry.

The Fouts called on fellow horseman Matt van der Woude, who is also a contractor, to reconstruct this essential room. "It was originally just a small space with no heat or storage," Matt reports. He added storage under a seat and a new thermal glass door for light and insulation.

According to Matt, Doug is in charge of vacuuming the house. The Fouts have installed a horse family's dream—a central vacuum system with kick plates in the kitchen and the mudroom. "All you have to do is sweep the dirt to the hole, kick it open, and step on the button," Matt says.

Matt incorporated other solutions for this family's hectic lifestyle into the design of the home. "Everyone is always on the run. It's all about speed, so I put up coat hooks and used high-gloss paint, which is easier to clean."

The kitchen renovation was done with an eye toward the few occasions on which the Fouts have guests. "We're outside all the time, but when we entertain, we do all the cooking," Beth says. They host an annual game dinner each February, at which venison, pheasant, dove, and duck are served.

"And if our guests want to socialize with us, they have to come to the kitchen," Beth says. For the kitchen remodel, they hired neighbors Charlie and Toni Gauthier, who specialize in custom kitchens. "We used to work

< 44 >

> "The Fouts have installed a horse family's dream—a central vacuum system with kick plates in the kitchen and the mudroom."

around an outdated center island with an old stove and old everything. Now I have a galley way, and the stove, cooktop, refrigerator, and sink are within two steps."

When they began the process of redesign, Beth met with the Gauthiers, showing them magazine articles with photos of kitchens she admired. She wanted a bay window seating area for family dinners and homework.

"My wife, Toni, came up with two or three drawings," Charlie says. "Then we met again and again. We took parts of drawings *a* and *d* and combined them with *b* and *c.* We kept modifying until we came up with a plan. For this lifestyle, the most important choice is the floor."

The Fouts chose a 12-inch-square ceramic tile in a soft shade of brown for the kitchen and the mudroom. "It's durable and doesn't take a lot of time and effort to clean," Charlie adds. "Hardwood floors wouldn't work here for the one time someone would bring mud inside. This is low maintenance. If it's dirty, you mop it with water. With hardwood in a high-traffic area, care and cleaning are more time-intensive."

PREVIOUS PAGE: Steeplechase trainer Doug Fout. CLOCKWISE FROM TOP RIGHT: All four members of the Fout family have at least two pairs of boots for riding and working in the barn. Caroline Fout is dressed to go hunting and pulls on a pair of paddock boots. The renovated kitchen provides storage space, ample wall space for photos from the racetrack and hunt fields, and a dining nook, which doubles as a perfect spot to do homework. A custom-made quilt in Caroline's bedroom features horse-show ribbons. The new mudroom has provided a place for hats, coats, and more photos. Bookshelves in the living room hold trophies.

National Steeplechase Association

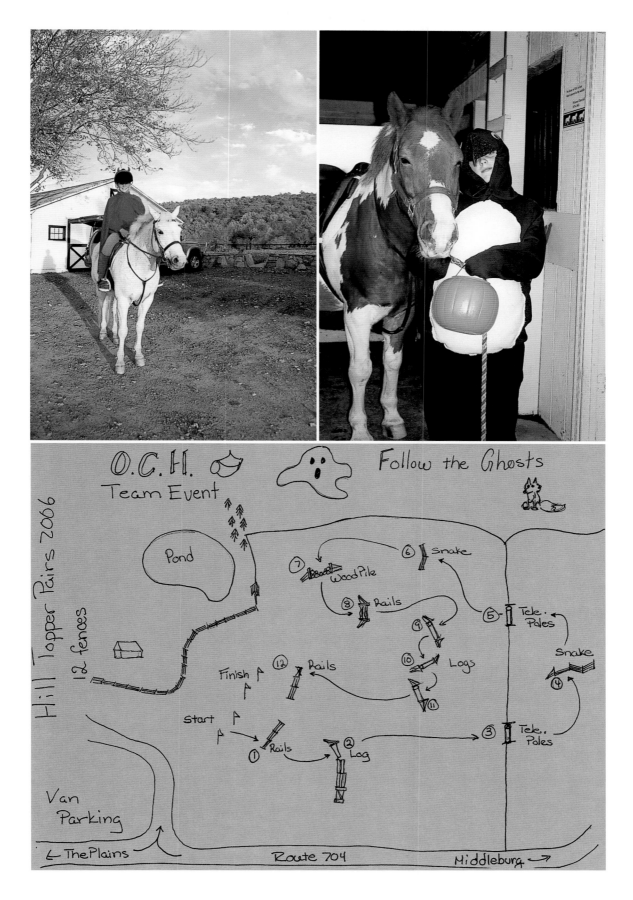

OPPOSITE: Caroline and Beth Fout. TOP, LEFT: Caroline Fout, dressed as a devil with a red cape and prepared to trick-or-treat on her pony, Candy. TOP, RIGHT: Her twin brother, Dunn, suited up as a penguin with his pony, Scout. ABOVE: Beth Fout drew the map of the course at the Orange County Hunt Team Chase event.

They enlarged the kitchen by pushing out 4 feet on one end, and Beth got her bay window seating area. There were several layers of decisions. Charlie would ask, "Where do you want to keep the canned goods? Where do you want to do the cooking?"

They reviewed many elements: What kind of cabinets—painted or stained? What type of countertops—Corian, limestone, laminated? The dishwasher—three cycles or six? On a trip to the appliance store they chose a refrigerator, a range, an oven, a microwave, a dishwasher, faucets, soap dispensers, and sinks, all in easy-care stainless steel. Beth wanted large cabinets with glass fronts for display and wall space for photos. "She also wanted a desk for the computer, a down-draft range, and double sinks," Charlie says. The old cabinets, which had five or six layers of paint, were replaced with custom-made cherry cabinets.

"To this day, I love the visual of the cabinets and the countertops," Beth says. "I've accomplished what I wanted."

LEFT, FROM TOP: One of the many traditions at the Upperville Colt and Horse Show each June is the family class, where Doug, Nina, Eve, Virginia, Beth, Dunn, and Caroline Fout remained in unison during the competition. The awards for the Orange County Team Chase included horse blankets, tack, and other goodies. The day begins at dawn at Doug Fout's training stables. OPPOSITE: Caroline Fout and Candy head over the log jump.

THE STEEPLECHASE SEASON

Look—the steeple!
I'll race you there for a cask of rum!
—Charles B. Parmer, *For Gold and Glory* (1939)

SPRING

Little Everglades, Dade City, Florida

Aiken Spring, Aiken, South Carolina

Carolina Cup, Camden, South Carolina

Stoneybrook, Raeford, North Carolina

Atlanta, Kingston, Georgia

My Lady's Manor, Monkton, Maryland

Strawberry Hill, New Kent, Virginia

Keeneland, Lexington, Kentucky

Block House, Tryon, North Carolina

Grand National, Butler, Maryland

Middleburg, Middleburg, Virginia

Foxfield Spring, Charlottesville, Virginia

Maryland Hunt Cup, Glyndon, Maryland

Queen's Cup, Mineral Springs, North Carolina

Virginia Gold Cup, The Plains, Virginia

Winterthur, Winterthur, Delaware

Iroquois, Nashville, Tennessee

Willowdale, Kennett Square, Pennsylvania

Radnor, Malvern, Pennsylvania

High Hope, Lexington, Kentucky

Fair Hill, Fair Hill, Maryland

SUMMER

Colonial Downs, New Kent, Virginia

Philadelphia Park, Bensalem, Pennsylvania

Saratoga, Saratoga Springs, New York

FALL

Shawan Downs, Hunt Valley, Maryland

Foxfield Fall, Charlottesville, Virginia

Virginia Fall, Middleburg, Virginia

Genesee Valley, Geneseo, New York

Morven Park, Leesburg, Virginia

Far Hills, Far Hills, New Jersey

International Gold Cup, The Plains, Virginia

Aiken Fall, Aiken, South Carolina

S'Chase at Callaway, Pine Mountain, Georgia

Montpelier, Montpelier Station, Virginia

Pennsylvania Hunt Cup, Unionville, Pennsylvania

Colonial Cup, Camden, South Carolina

For details: www.nationalsteeplechase.com

THE WOLFS AND
THEIR HORSES

Elizabeth and Bill Wolf begin planning their annual Holiday Hunt Breakfast months in advance. They sort through books and art auction catalogs, searching for appropriate artwork to use on the invitation. A hint of the refined ambiance of the party arrives in the mail as a save-the-date card six weeks prior to the early December event; the card always includes a foxhunting scene.

A pair of mixed green wreaths with red bows greets guests at the entrance to the Wolfs' Somerset Farm, near Middleburg, Virginia. This area is a mecca for many well-known equestrians, including Olympic gold medal winners Joe Fargis and David O'Connor and the late Pamela Harriman, Paul Mellon, and Jacqueline Kennedy Onassis. The Wolfs have set the stage for the Piedmont Hunt to gather.

A Della Robbia garland of cedar and magnolia, studded with apples, pomegranates, and pineapple and punctuated with red silk shantung bows, graces the entrance portico of the main stone house and adds a festive holiday note as riders and foxhounds reunite. A coordinating 30-inch wreath is hung on the front door.

After a two-, three-, five-, or even six-hour jaunt through the fields, leaping over stone walls and galloping through streams, the riders return cold and famished. They are not, however, in the least bit tired. Rather, they are eager to exchange tales, much as golfers do when they return to the clubhouse after a remarkable round of eighteen holes.

The hunt breakfast is a misnomer; it never takes place

in the morning. The late lunch buffet at the Wolfs' features grilled beef tenderloin served with horseradish sauce; grilled salmon with Mediterranean sauce, orzo, and diced vegetables; and bow-tie pasta with tomato sauce. A children's table offers chicken fingers, baby carrots with dip, cookies, and brownies. The grown-up dessert tray spills over with French pastries, lemon squares, and pecan cookies.

The two-hundred-plus guests include nonriding friends and neighbors. As they mingle and munch, their eyes cannot help but be drawn to the centerpiece on the table, a handsome 22-inch-high bronze sculpture called *Spirit of Competition,* made by Elizabeth, an accomplished sculptor and equestrian.

The sculpture is surrounded by pears, pomegranates, sprigs of holly, and cream-colored velvet roses, installed by floral designers Deborah Graham and Amy Sullivan of Country Way in downtown Middleburg. Elizabeth's artistic touch on the flanking pair of three-light Sheffield candelabras incorporates a simple solitary apple-green candle merged with textured cream-colored candles wrapped with threads of green.

Elizabeth and Bill were married in May 1999, and their home now overflows with examples of their mutual love of art. "She's taught me the details and pleasures of art," says Bill, an orthopedic surgeon. "It grabs you, the work that it takes."

One of those examples hangs above the mantel in the dining room. The mantel itself spills over with bay laurel

< 55 >

leaves, magnolia, and more cream-colored velvet roses to echo the centerpiece. Old-fashioned round glass ornaments in cream and apple green and touches of faux silver-dollar-plant sprigs with a pearl garland woven throughout finalize the rococo profusion. All of this is to set off and honor the allegorical painting by Jean-Jacques Bachelier, *The Horse and the Wolf,* inspired by a fable of the same name.

The horse has a hurt hoof and, in the fable, the wolf claims he can help him: "I have the honor to attend your race, and am a surgeon, too, the whole world knows." After the horse gives the wolf a swift kick that makes "a marmalade of teeth and jaws," the Wolf concludes: "Well done! Each one should stick to his own trade. My claws were made for butchery, not herb-collecting."

Elizabeth and Bill frequently search out art to purchase. While on vacation in Jackson, Wyoming, something caught their eyes as they strolled down Center Street.

"First of all, we have thirty-nine horses at home, so what do we do on vacation? We go to a dude ranch," Bill notes with a smile. "Then we visit the galleries." Floyd Tennison DeWitt's sculpture *The Golden Cayuse* stopped them in their tracks. The gleaming horse statue is a tribute to the mixed-blood Cayuse horses used by cowboys in the West and named after a tribe of Native Americans with legendary expertise around horses. DeWitt, now in his seventies, rode horses while growing up on the untamed Montana plains. He always admired the Western-inspired art of C. M. Russell and Frederick Remington, and it has been said DeWitt could handle "the most ornery beast in the corral."

ABOVE: The Piedmont Fox Hounds gather at Somerset Farm. OPPOSITE: Bill Wolf greets members of the hunt at the portico of his home, which has been festooned with a Della Robbia garland of cedar and magnolia with apples, pomegranates, and pineapple accented by red silk shantung bows.

CLOCKWISE FROM TOP LEFT: Floyd Tennison DeWitt's sculpture *The Inheritor II*. Elizabeth Wolf's sculpture *Spirit of Competition* is the hunt breakfast centerpiece in the dining room, where decorator Jean Perin had the walls upholstered in Scalamandré fabric and Bachelier's *The Horse and the Wolf* hangs above the mantel. Sculptor Floyd Tennison DeWitt's *The Golden Cayuse*. In the den, the Wolfs' love of horses and dogs is evident everywhere. The ottoman, now covered in a Cowtan & Tout fabric, was purchased at auction in New Orleans. Elizabeth Wolf's bronzes on the antique wood tray are *Bath* and *Cooling Out*. Rose Cummings fabrics were used for the curtains.

The Wolfs could not resist *The Golden Cayuse,* which is the only version of this bronze sculpture gilded in 22-carat gold leaf.

Inside the gallery, Elizabeth and Bill spotted another DeWitt sculpture, *The Inheritor II.* The artist says it was inspired by a Roman statue of Marcus Aurelius, who pursued harmony. The Wolfs decided to purchase both pieces, which are now in perfect harmony in the great room of their elegant home.

"Because we are a nation of so many varying nationalities, this sculpture is intended to celebrate the vast and complex diversity which is America," the artist once said. "*The Golden Cayuse* becomes my personal metaphor for all Americans, and addresses the wild, untamed nature of a nation still struggling to discover its true spiritual identity."

The Golden Cayuse stands unobtrusively in one corner of the great room, and *The Inheritor II* sits on a table behind a sofa, but Elizabeth and Bill alternate the placement of the two sculptures to give each its due.

A 10-foot Christmas tree placed in another corner of the room is adorned with a multicolored compilation of homemade, vintage, and new ornaments in equestrian motifs: a fox in a scarlet riding jacket, a glass jockey in blue silks, a pair of bright green Wellington boots, a gentleman in a top hat on a brown horse with a sly fox riding along behind.

As the party winds down and the guests depart, they pass by the barns. Each horse has his own stocking, to be filled with carrots and molasses-encrusted oat treats. After all, the Wolfs' horses deserve to be treated to a hunt breakfast, too.

IF THESE WALLS COULD TALK

Decorator Jean Perin brought in artist Martitia "Tish" Inman from Gallatin, Tennessee, to paint and finish the walls of the Wolfs' home. Tish's repertoire encompasses faux finishes from tortoiseshell to rich green malachite and deep blue lapis.

Tish glazed the walls in the Wolfs' den and great room. In the den, she began the process by applying a base color of red latex. Next, she mixed a series of glazes, starting with a darker color. "Then I added two or three more coats, and each time the color got lighter," she says. "I like to say the final coat mellowed it out." Tish used a brush with 5-inch-long natural bristles to drag the glaze vertically. "It's a simple technique," she says. This created a perpendicular appearance, making the standard 8-foot ceilings appear higher. Another ingredient contributes to the vertical illusion in the den: The Wolfs had every inch of wall space calculated so that they could have the crown molding designed and cut to take up a larger area on the ceiling than it does on the wall, where many of their paintings now hang.

In the great room, Tish started with a basic undercoat of yellow. "Each coat of glaze added was intended to mist over or fuzz it out," she says. In both rooms, the artwork is the focal point. "The walls should not outshine the paintings," Tish adds.

Sitting in the red den, Bill Wolf observed:
'What I collect from any artistic standpoint is not academic, it's emotional.
Each painting or bronze stands alone for me.'

Part II: On the Farm

FARM LIFE MEANS MORE THAN

the day-to-day tasks of caring for horses and cleaning up after them. In southern Florida, a pet miniature donkey resides in a barn that resembles an Addison Mizner–designed villa one might see along Route A1A in nearby Palm Beach.

For some people, "the farm" conjures images of sweeping vistas of rolling green pastures and handsome old weathered barns. History repeats itself in Virginia as curious horses stick their necks out to explore the passing bustle, not knowing that another pair of champion horses in a previous generation was captured in the same pose in a cherished family portrait on the very same farm.

In Maryland, trophies, photos, and mementos of a five-time Horse of the Year are preserved in a renovated post office along with a private collection of equestrian-inspired needlepoint chairs, pillows, and valances created by an equestrienne who was an icon in her day.

On chilly, misty mornings in Kentucky, a former Kentucky Derby winner retired to stud relishes a second career in a pristine landscape reminiscent of a college campus that is actually a working farm.

OPPOSITE, CLOCKWISE FROM TOP RIGHT: Ouisha McKinney's sketch provides inspiration for her custom-designed sweaters. Rigan McKinney was the leading gentleman jockey in 1933, '34, '36, and '38. Kelso's yellow satin ribbon. Five-time Horse of the Year Kelso retired to an 8-acre paddock at Woodstock Farm. The 240-year-old McKinney home in Kentucky is filled with antique horse prints. Calumet Farm in Lexington. Foxhunting at teatime. Smarty Jones is the big man on campus. CENTER: A vendor at the Saratoga racetrack offers artwork created on the spot.

<64>

WILD WHINNY
FARM

Françoise Rambach started riding horses as a teenager in Belgium. As a young career woman, she moved to New York City, where in the late 1970s she met and married Harvey Rambach, a raw materials chemical dealer.

The Rambachs lived on Park Avenue and shared a love of art, collecting American Modernists active from 1914 to 1940, including Alfred Steiglitz, Georgia O'Keeffe, Arthur Dove, and Marsden Hartley, among others. A 224-page catalog of their artwork was published in 1991 in connection with an exhibition at the Gerald Peters Gallery in New York. It included a detailed listing of their impressive collection that ran to fifty-one pages.

"When we sold that collection in 1999, our home was very empty," Françoise recalls—at least until Harvey purchased a large horse sculpture by William Zorach, a Lithuanian-American sculptor and artist (1887–1966), that was done in 1938. "That's the piece Harvey bought at Sotheby's. When it came home, I told Harvey to buy me the farm that goes with it."

Zorach's work can be seen in Boston at the Museum of Fine Arts and in Washington, D.C., at the National Gallery of Art and at The Phillips Collection. Visitors to Manhattan can see Zorach's *Pegasus* at the Whitney Museum and his *Spirit of the Dance* at Radio City Music Hall. His sculpture is recognized for its uncomplicated density and purified conformation.

Harvey eventually indulged his wife's wish, and they purchased a farm in Middletown Township, New Jersey, where Françoise returned to riding horses. They also

began to collect art again, this time to reflect some of their many animals. "We started with livestock and animal prints. We bought a few in New York. And then we became a little obsessed and spent time in London, where we bought most of our prints," Françoise notes.

Their prints of "British Farm Livestock" date from 1780 to 1910, with many of them published in *Farmer's* magazine as advertisements for animals. In those days, there was a craze for rotund animals—the fatter the better—as weight was considered a sign of good health. When the owners of these animals wanted to advertise them, they asked the artist to vastly exaggerate their already big appearance. As a result, the owner is often depicted as smaller than his cow, horse, sheep, or pig.

The Rambachs began to find the harsh New Jersey winters difficult, so in 2005 they moved to Palm Beach County, Florida, full-time. They built a Flemish-style farmhouse in homage to Françoise's love of her native Belgium. They named it Wild Whinny Farm in honor of Sebastian, the resident miniature donkey.

As guests enter the great room, a 7-by-6-foot profile of a white horse leaps from over the mantel in a work of graphite on canvas by Joseph Piccillo. Born in Buffalo in 1941, Piccillo is noted for his irreproachable images of horses. "I find it very rare to see horse paintings devoid of any sentimentality. That was the attraction for me," Françoise relates. "It just showed the animal in all its beauty and strength."

'Harvey indulges my love of horses with amusement,' says Françoise. 'And he encourages me to continue to improve my riding. I know it's silly, but these horses and my five rescued dogs make my happiness. To see the horses lazily grazing or scratching each other's back or to hear them whinny when they see me come with a carrot warms my heart.'

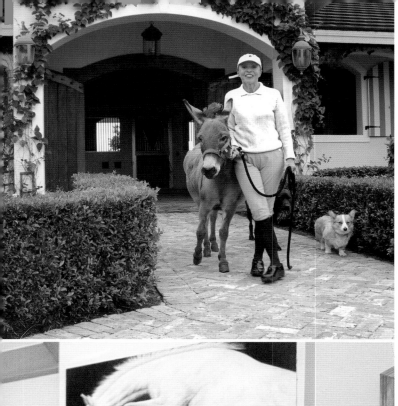

CARE OF PAINTINGS

According to Don Williams, the senior conservator at the Smithsonian Museum Conservation Institute in Washington, D.C., the three main causes of damage to paintings are light, temperature, and humidity. "Bugs, air pollutants, and humans also cause harm," he says.

Light is the origin of the most ruin. "Ultraviolet light from the sun or unfiltered UV-emitting fluorescent lamps should never fall on the surface of a painting," he cautions in his book, *Saving Stuff*.

Don advises against lighting paintings by attaching a fixture to the frame, which distributes light unevenly over the picture and can generate too much heat in the center. He suggests using fiber-optic lighting or mounting incandescent floodlights far enough from the art so as not to subject it to too much heat.

OPPOSITE: Horses can be schooled near the patio area at Wild Whinny Farm. LEFT: The Rambachs' collection of prints of British farm livestock on the far wall dates from 1780; artist Joseph Piccillo's graphite on canvas over the mantel measures 6 by 7 feet. TOP: Françoise Rambach with farm mascot Sebastian. ABOVE: Harvey and Françoise Rambach's Flemish-style farmhouse.

WELL BUILT

Barns and stables around the world span an architectural spectrum from the ultrafancy Royal Mews in London and the Moorish-inspired structures at the Real Escuela Andaluza del Arte Ecuestre in Seville, Spain, to the minimalist refined former tobacco barns in Kentucky. "The horses don't know if they're living in the Taj Mahal or on skid row," says Don Stewart, a trainer and nationally recognized horse show judge from Ocala, Florida. "A horse can look good walking out of any barn if it is conditioned properly. They need to be fed and taken care of; that's the vital part of the equation."

THE BLUEGRASS STATE

Each spring in Lexington, Kentucky, yellow forsythia bursts like popcorn, white jonquils dance in the gentle breeze, and dogwood trees punctuate the season in shades of white and pink.

At the corner of New Circle Road and Versailles Road, dozens of foals can be seen taking a midmorning nap in the sunshine at Calumet Farm. Their tiny fuzzy tails twitch at the flies while the mares graze nearby on that legendary bluegrass. The white barns are trimmed with red—a nod to the Calumet Farm racing colors, which include devil's red.

A drive past the many Thoroughbred farms—Darby Dan, Gainesway, and Clovelly—on Georgetown Pike, Newtown Pike, and Versailles Road makes obvious that the sheer multitude of these sweet foals means serious business. The vernacular of the barns and stables incor-

porates a blend of historic designs, with the well-being of the horse always a paramount consideration.

Down the road in Paris, the Hancock family at Claiborne Farm has been breeding horses for the racetrack since 1915. On these grounds, 1941 Triple Crown winner Whirlaway, eight-time sire-of-the-year Bold Ruler, and 1973 Triple Crown winner Secretariat stood at stud. There are now fourteen stallions in residence.

The distinguished board-and-batten black wood barns that dot the fields at Claiborne originally held tobacco. When tobacco leaves were curing, the tall, slim doors along the sides of the barn were opened for ventilation; now opening them serves the same purpose for the horses. A one-story shed attached to the barn functioned as an area where workers stripped leaves from the tobacco.

Workers tied up the tobacco into a fistful, which translated into a unit of measurement called a *hand*. This universal calculation also refers to the height of a horse. A smallish horse runs about 15 hands; larger horses measure as much as 17 hands.

A large barn, which once held carriages, has also been converted with stalls. A U-shaped yearling barn with a courtyard is built of cinder block. The philosophy here is simple and utilitarian. The sheds and outbuildings have tin fish-scale shingles that have aged beautifully. Each barn is numbered in the unlikely event of a "freakish fire," says Dell Hancock, or the more likely occasion when the veterinarian or blacksmith pays a visit.

For large commercial Thoroughbred farms, the most

important consideration is efficiency, according to Joe Martinolich, head of the equine studio CMW, an architectural firm in Lexington. The layout must be organized so the grooms can turn the horses out in the paddocks and get back in quickly. "The farm managers have the schedules down to the minute," he relates. If it takes a recreational rider twenty minutes to bring a favorite horse into the barn, that is considered acceptable, but in the horse business, time is money.

Joe also designed the extravagant barns at Gainsborough Farm, owned by Darley, the international horse operation of Sheikh Mohammed bin Rashid Al Maktoum, the ruler of Dubai. The octagonal stallion barn has an impressive vaulted core intended to serve as an area for showing off the stallions. The stalls are also octagonal. There is just one thing: Horses no longer live inside this particular barn. Instead, the building is used for charity events such as a cocktail party and auction for the Bluegrass Conservancy (a nonprofit land trust), and the Woodford Humane Society Freedom Fest, for which the stalls are magically transformed with designer table-tops and nooks. The natural light from the clerestory windows on the upper level and the lantern on top floods the area.

The objective, according to the architect, was to "achieve a high level of architectural elegance by combining fine materials, careful detailing, and a unique yet functional design." The high-end components include brick and granite aisle flooring, extensive windows, and brass-trimmed stall fronts.

PREVIOUS PAGE, ABOVE: The Moorish-inspired stables at the Real Escuela Andaluza del Arte Ecuestre in Seville, Spain. PREVIOUS PAGE, BELOW: A more modest shelter, in the United States. CLOCKWISE FROM ABOVE RIGHT: The newer stables at Spendthrift Farm have solid brass accessories. The tall octagonal barn at Darley Gainsborough Farm was designed with a vaulted central core for an infusion of natural lighting. Visitors inspect a yearling at Claiborne Farm. The bright yellow racing colors at Claiborne can be seen throughout the stables. Springtime brings a new crop of potential Kentucky Derby winners. Kentucky Bluegrass. CENTER: The stalls at Darley Gainsborough are transformed by local interior designers for the Woodford County Humane Society Freedom Fest.

THE OLD DOMINION

In Virginia, the late philanthropist Paul Mellon, a life-long devotee of Thoroughbred racing with six champions and one hundred stakes winners to his credit, built several stables at his Rokeby Farm. The broodmares and their foals live in a British-inspired courtyard barn designed by H. Page Cross and Son of New York. A bronze sculpture by John Skeaping of the horse Mill Reef, winner of the Epsom Derby, the Prix de l'Arc de Triomphe, and the Queen Elizabeth II Diamond Stakes, is the centerpiece.

The mares and foals at Rokeby live in spacious stalls, 15 feet square, with fresh straw stacked ankle deep. The wooden buckets and wheelbarrows are made in a carpenter's workshop on the other side of the farm. The wheelbarrows are designed to fit perfectly in the stall door opening so a foal cannot slip out while the stall is being cleaned. An overhead heat lamp adds warmth for newborns, who usually arrive in the frigid months of January and February—and most often in the middle of the night. The glass windows, which may seem hazardous, are deliberately set back to prevent injury from broken glass.

OPPOSITE: At Claiborne Farm the pathway was aligned on a direct axis with the barn. ABOVE: The British-inspired stables were built in 1949 by the late Paul Mellon at Rokeby Farm in Upperville, Virginia.

THE GOLDEN STATE

Due to a simple lack of space, horse owners near Burbank, California, do not have the luxury of turning their horses out to romp and play in spacious paddocks. Some owners even keep their horses in the backyard near the Los Angeles Equestrian Center and Griffith Park in the Burbank Rancho neighborhood, which is zoned for horses. Crosswalks feature elevated traffic-control buttons so mounted riders can easily reach over to push them.

In August 1924, humorist and cowboy at heart Will Rogers wrote, "A man that don't love a horse, there is something the matter with him." This quote is now etched on the cornerstone of the mule barn at his ranch near Pacific Palisades.

This board-and-batten open-style barn had a tar-paper roof and was intended for mules, which were used to pull equipment on the 186-acre ranch. During the 1932 Olympic Games in Los Angeles, the Japanese equestrian team boarded its horses here. The original mule barn, known as Jim's Barn in honor of Will Rogers's son, who enjoyed riding and roping, was torn down in the early 1940s. The Will Rogers Cooperative Association rebuilt the structure and rededicated it on March 25, 2006.

The largest stable now on the property is the green timber-frame main barn, where Will Rogers and his friends would rope and ride. It's actually two separate stables brought to the ranch from the San Fernando Valley and reconnected to an imposing riding rotunda. The doors to the rotunda are built on a radius to fit on the circular building. A louvered clerestory along the roofline was way ahead of its time in aiding ventilation. Grooms' quarters, a saddle room, and a wash stall complete the building's amenities.

Will Rogers's ranch is now a state park and listed on the National Register of Historic Places. Horses continue to be a vital part of ranch life, which includes riding lessons and polo games.

LEFT, FROM TOP: The owners of these horses live in the adjacent wing. Some horses in California live in the backyard. Some horses live in the lap of luxury. OPPOSITE, ABOVE: The barns at the Will Rogers Ranch have a round training pen in the center. OPPOSITE, BELOW: At Rokeby Farm the wooden water barrels are handmade in a workroom on the property.

A STITCH IN TIME

Helene Allaire Crozer of Philadelphia was a recent graduate of a Swiss boarding school and a daring champion glider pilot in the mid-1930s when she met and married fellow flying enthusiast Richard C. duPont. A member of the well-to-do chemical manufacturing clan from Wilmington, Delaware, he was equally adventurous. They crossed the Atlantic in the *Hindenburg,* and she once flew a plane under the Chesapeake City Bridge, not far from where they had settled in Maryland at Woodstock Farm.

After Richard duPont was killed in a gliding accident in 1943, Mrs. duPont never remarried. She devoted her life to bringing up their two children, Richard Jr. and Lana, preserving the Cecil County countryside, rescuing abused animals, and raising Angus cattle.

Mrs. duPont always rode horses, but it wasn't until the late 1950s that her pursuit of success in Thoroughbred racing commenced. Her horse, Ambehaving, was her first big stakes winner, and then along came Kelso, the horse that changed her life.

The small (15.1-hand) dark bay horse was described by his trainers as headstrong, leaving no option but to geld the peevish colt. Even then, Kelso had the constant companionship of two dogs, Sketch and Mickey; later, another dog, named Charlie Potatoes, slept near Kelso's head. The horse was bedded on sugarcane shavings, and his sweet tooth was legendary. There were even private-label sugar cubes wrapped in Kelso paper.

Kelso was Horse of the Year five times (1960–1964) and winner of nearly $2 million. When he retired to an 8-acre paddock at Woodstock, he received hundreds of letters each week—Mrs. duPont gave him his own mailbox. One boy wrote: "Dear Kelso, God put us here at the same time, you to be a great racehorse, and me to be a good boy for my mother and father. Good luck in 1965. John Price Easterburn Acres, Wilm.8, Del."

Kelso's best-known fan was Heather Noble, a teenager from Alexandria, Virginia, who wore yellow and gray racing colors to school on the days "Kelly" was running. She wrote a song called "Hello, Kelso," set to the tune of "Hello, Dolly." She taught her pet parakeet, Hazel, to chirp "Win, Kelso."

While some racehorse owners would simply turn their horses out to pasture for a long retirement, Mrs. duPont loved to ride Kelso both cross-country and foxhunting. She also played golf and tennis and swam in the Bohemia River, which runs along the southern edge of the farm. She took a dip with the dolphins in the Florida Keys decades before it became a tourist destination.

Despite all her outdoor activity, she also was a heavy smoker. In an effort to stop, Mrs. duPont began in 1940 to feverishly turn out masses of vibrant needlepoint canvases. For the next six decades, she created pillows, purses, valances, and chair covers in patterns of flora and fauna—including, of course, horses.

Her most elaborate work was a rug in forty-eight sections, each one in memory of a horse, a dog, or one of her ninety formerly stray cats (all of which she had spayed or neutered). She incorporated images of her homes in

<79>

Delaware and the Virgin Islands and her children's favorite pony, Christopher Columbus. The completed piece measured 9 by 15 feet.

Mrs. duPont finished needlepoint seats for a pair of chairs made from cherry trees that were taken down at St. Andrew's School, which was founded by her father-in-law, Felix duPont, in 1928 in Middletown, Delaware. She donated many pieces to be auctioned for some of her favorite charities: Paws for Life, Mid-Atlantic Horse Rescue, Greener Pastures, Thoroughbred Charities of America, and Union Hospital in Chesapeake City.

Mrs. duPont ordered her needlepoint supplies from a shop called Mazaltov on Madison Avenue in New York City. Artist Rita Klein designed and painted many of her canvases and later opened her own shop. The two women formed an artistic bond. Mrs. duPont would call the shop to discuss a concept, and Rita went to work on it shortly thereafter. The canvases were twelve tiny squares to the inch. A calculated supply of Persian wool accompanied each fabrication.

"She liked corals and reds," Rita says, adding, "She was not a lavender and purple girl. Mrs. duPont worked in the traditional basket-weave stitch. Her needlework was her constant companion. She kept it in a little basket and took it everywhere."

Her last order to Rita came just weeks before her death on January 6, 2006, at age ninety-two. Not long after, Mrs. duPont's daughter, Lana, began sorting through her things. Some of the needlepoint pieces had been eaten by moths, so Lana began a meticulous restoration process. The office at Woodstock Farm, originally a post office building in Odessa, Delaware, that Mrs. duPont had relocated and adapted, now houses many treasured needlepoint creations along with Kelso's trophies, blankets, and memorabilia.

PREVIOUS PAGES: The legacy of Kelso remains, as seen in silver trophies, paintings, and the beautiful needlepoint valances, pillows, and chairs sewn by his late owner, Allaire duPont. CLOCKWISE FROM TOP: Bohemia Stables' racing colors. Many of the needlepoint chairs done by Mrs. duPont are fox and hound related. Lana duPont (also pictured at center, with her dogs) brought Kelso to the Washington International Horse Show for an exhibition in 1968. Kelso is buried at Woodstock Farm. Kelso won the Jockey Club Gold Cup. An old post office building from Odessa, Delaware, serves as the offices at Woodstock Farm. Allaire duPont rode Kelso cross-country after he retired from racing. Five-time Horse of the Year, Kelso was named for Allaire duPont's close friend Kelso Alsop Everett and not for the town in Scotland of the same name.

WELL WORN

In Kentucky, where breeding and background are revered, the 143-acre Stony Point Farm, owned by the McKinney family, oozes history and horses. The 240-year-old whitewashed brick colonial main house is on the National Register of Historic Places and is filled with family memorabilia.

In 1962, Ohio sportsman Rigan McKinney purchased Stony Point Farm and brought to it his fifth wife, the former Frances Warfield of Howard County, Maryland. Frances was a skilled horsewoman whose mother was a master of foxhounds. The McKinneys raised seven children.

Rigan was the nation's leading gentleman jockey for four seasons: 1933, 1934, 1936, and 1938. He had a record 128 wins as an amateur steeplechase rider. Rigan went on to be a top trainer and Thoroughbred breeder and was inducted into the National Museum of Racing Hall of Fame in 1968.

The McKinneys summered on the Delaware shore and sold yearlings at the sales in Saratoga. In between, they mastered horsemanship, and when they entered the horse-show ring for the family class, they outnumbered all others and cut a stylish swath.

The family spent winters at Lake Tahoe, where Frances homeschooled her brood and honed their skiing skills. Five of the seven McKinney children made the national ski team. The youngest, Tamara, was a member of the U.S. Olympic ski team in 1980, 1984, and 1988.

Both parents have passed on, and the original clan is down to five. Laura McKinney and Sheila McKinney run a horse business at Stony Point Farm, and Ouisha McKinney pitches in part-time.

When Ouisha is not helping out on the farm, she designs equestrian-style knitwear and hand-painted earthenware. "I have always been crafty and love making and fixing things," she begins. "When I was ten years old, I made a paper collage, and I said, 'When I grow up, I'm going to paint.'"

Her foray into art and design began when her sister Tamara was on the Olympic ski team. Ouisha made colorful ski hats for all the team members. "Mom taught me to knit when I was five and then I took it up again at sixteen," says Ouisha, who had finished high school the previous year. "I bought a book about how to knit on a loom. It had seventeen lessons. I did the first six and never looked back," she says.

Ouisha sold her hats to other skiers who were clamoring for them. In 1981, she took her hats and sweaters to the Devon Horse Show. She sold out the first day.

Many of her creations have strong primary colors with soft accents of flowers and blossoms in teal, cream, and fawn. She incorporates horses, foxes, Welsh corgis, and Jack Russells in fibers of wool, cotton, and viscose chenille.

More than half of her sweaters are custom designed. A horse owner might want his or her racing colors incorporated into a pullover, or a dog lover might want a favorite Jack Russell on the front or back of a cardi-

< 8 4 >

gan. For these, Ouisha begins by taking measurements and making notes before moving forward with a sketch.

Ouisha's talents also extend to painting. Her line of bisque ware includes mugs, plates, large bowls, and a popular Christmas ornament of a rocking horse. All are painted with an underglaze, then dipped in a clear glaze before being fired in a kiln for twenty hours.

In the studio in her condo near the family farm are pots of paints in morning-glory blue, brick red, and Irish green. A vibrant display of hats and sweaters takes over what was supposed to be a dining room.

Three cats, Banshee, Minnie Muon, and Bobby Bobcat, curl up on one corner of a utility table as Ouisha works full tilt. An old photograph of the McKinney family riding their horses is on a nearby table. Ouisha has been in Kentucky for so many years that some mistake her for a lifelong resident. She is quick to smile and point out, "We live in Kentucky, but we are not of Kentucky."

LEFT, FROM TOP: Ouisha, Laura, and Sheila McKinney take a break from their morning barn chores. Rigan McKinney, with Mrs. Avrell Clark and Henry Bull, was the nation's leading gentleman jockey during the 1930s. Ouisha McKinney's dining room table overflows with her hand-painted bowls and plates. OPPOSITE, CLOCKWISE FROM ABOVE RIGHT: Ouisha wears one of her own designs. According to historians, the brick house was built during the 1790s by John Parker as a main house to replace an earlier log house. Ouisha's foray into art and design began when she supplied ski caps for the Olympic ski team. Horses of all shapes and sizes can be found at the McKinney home. Rigan McKinney's trophies are displayed in the entry hall.

EQUESTRIAN FASHION

On a brisk evening in December 1984, three distinguished gentlemen dressed in formal scarlet foxhunting regalia walked down Fifth Avenue in New York City. Masters of Foxhounds Paul Mellon, Ambassador Charles Whitehouse, and James Young were going for drinks at the apartment of Jacqueline Kennedy Onassis before the gala opening of the Man and the Horse exhibit at the Metropolitan Museum of Art.

The legendary fashion connoisseur Diana Vreeland, editor emeritus at *Harper's Bazaar* and *Vogue*, was the special consultant for the extravaganza mounted by the Costume Institute. Mrs. Vreeland extolled the accoutrements of the horse: shining spurs, colorful racing silks, and calfskin boots, and at the same time said: "One dresses down to perfection."

"One dresses not for display but to meet the inspiration of the ideal," she wrote in the introduction of the accompanying book. "The splendid attire of the world of the horse is the fulfillment of man's half of a covenant."

The simple and somewhat militaristic trappings of the horse have stirred designers for hundreds of years. Designer and avid equestrian Coco Chanel patterned her own pair of jodhpurs upon a pair borrowed from a male groom.

What many who walk down Fifth Avenue wearing a pair of Gucci loafers with a bass snaffle bit do not know is that the house of Gucci began in the early 1900s as a saddle shop and expanded with leather accessories. The distinctive red and green webbing first used on handbags (with a bamboo handle) was inspired by the overgirth used on saddles.

Years later, the loafers were elevated to a status symbol and motivated numerous designers to incorporate the iconic image of the snaffle bit on everything from dresses to ties, not to mention a trunkload of knockoffs.

For anyone looking for equestrian-style clothing, the boutiques at the horse shows and tack shops have items that cannot be found in major department stores—tweed hacking jackets, needlepoint belts with horses, and scarves and ties, to name just a few. "Tailors, bootmakers, and hatmakers alike know that men and women will never look as good as they do in their riding gear," Mrs. Vreeland wrote.

> " The legendary fashion connoisseur Diana Vreeland extolled the accoutrements of the horse: shining spurs, colorful racing silks, and calfskin boots. And designer and avid equestrian Coco Chanel patterned her own pair of jodhpurs upon a pair borrowed from a male groom. "

ALL IN THE FAMILY

Sharon Maloney walked into a friend's home one day in 2003 and recognized a painting on the wall. "It had been in our house all my life," she relates. "When I came home, I asked my mother about it. She told me she had donated it to the SPCA auction and bazaar."

It turned out the painting was by Wesley Dennis, a local artist best known as the illustrator of the famous children's tale *Misty of Chincoteague*. Mrs. Maloney was a patron of many local artists and many local charities.

For her part, Sharon Maloney inherited not only a love of art and antiques but also of horses and dogs. Her home on the back part of the family's Dogpatch Farm in Warrenton, Virginia, is filled with exquisite old paintings, including several pieces by Wesley Dennis. Sets of china, silver trophies won by the family's race- and show horses, and photos of her father abound.

A 1943 win photo shows John Maloney receiving a silver tray after his horse Resolute II captured the Dangerfield Handicap at the Jamaica racetrack on Long Island. The very same silver tray is now casually propped up next to the photo.

The Maloneys were married in 1945 and settled in Warrenton. Sharon Maloney was just a little girl when her father died in 1955. Mrs. Maloney raised Sharon and her brothers, Kevin and John T. ("Chip"), with an emphasis on deriving joy from life in the country—riding ponies, swimming, jumping on a trampoline.

The main house was constantly filled with friends of her children, many of whom called Mrs. Maloney "Aunt Betty."

The attic was converted to a dormitory, with rows of beds for overnight stays by members of what became their extended family. This accommodation continued even as many of the Maloneys' friends went off to college, started their careers, married, and even bounced back after a divorce.

Dogpatch Farm remained a gathering place, and friends continue to flock from miles around on the first Saturday in May. After they watch the Kentucky Derby, the party goes on into the wee hours. If the dormitory is overbooked, there is always the trampoline.

The farm is a retreat for animals as well as friends. Betty Maloney, who died in 2006 at age eighty-nine, had a soft spot in her heart for dogs and was a founder of the local animal shelter, which was housed on the property for thirty-two years.

Mrs. Maloney put on small horse shows to raise funds for the shelter. Everyone had a task: setting up the jumps, mowing the grass, manning the refreshment stand.

Mrs. Maloney was a champion hunter rider and won countless trophies. The engraved handle of a walking cane that opens into a stick for measuring the height of horses reveals it to be a first-place award at the 1938 Piping Rock Horse Show on Long Island. A painting of her two best horses, Prompt Payment and Substitution, hangs over the mantel in the living room. The two bays are sticking their heads out of the stalls in a dark green board-and-batten barn at Dogpatch that is still very much in use today. Artist Jean Bowman, who lived in

PREVIOUS PAGES, LEFT: An eighteenth-century tiger maple Chippendale slant-front desk holds family photos, antiques, books, and trophies. The painting hanging above of the British champion race horse Ormonde with F. Archer is attributed to H. Hall. OPPOSITE: A circa 1880 English earthenware blue Pearlware jug. TOP: Artist Jean Bowman painted the portrait of the Maloney horses in the barn around 1950. ABOVE: Fifty years later the horse tradition continues at Dogpatch Farm.

the area, executed the painting.

Sharon has integrated many of her mother's pieces into her own cottage. A set of whimsical miniature Vienna bronzes of foxes playing musical instruments dates from 1880. A pair of painted cast-iron jockey bookends from the 1950s clutches a set of faux book covers. Inside the leather cases is a collection of 1912 one-cent postcards her grandfather collected in his travels: Historic Boston, From the Mountains to the Sea, The Land of Sunshine, and Missions of the Southwest.

She has collected cobalt blue jasperware with white bas-relief hunting scenes around the center of each piece. The pieces, displayed on a marble side table in her bathroom, date from the 1880s and were made by the British companies Copeland, Hall, and Wedgwood.

Sharon has traveled to England and around the United States in search of additional pieces. She acquired so many, she started her own part-time antique business, though her full-time pursuit involves horses. She works with up to thirty Thoroughbreds, much like her father did, breaking yearlings, training two-year-olds, and caring for other horses in need of rest and rehabilitation.

A 1975 win photo of Sharon's horse Virginia Fats at Saratoga hangs on the wall of the main house. Matt Collins, an original member of the extended family, did the brightly colored primitive painting of a horse called Kitty Tatch in the winner's circle, which holds a place of honor in the family room. Like her mother, Sharon Maloney appreciates fine art; like her father, she has a knack for making it to the winner's circle.

FRAMING AND HANGING

The frames on fine art are to be admired nearly as much as the paintings themselves. "The frame should bring the painting to life," says decorator and designer Jimmie Emmett of Upperville, Virginia. "A frame can also kill a painting. A heavy rococo frame on a primitive painting does not work. You would need something early, an ebonized frame with a color rub."

Art aficionados study the history of frames as well as paintings. Carver Thomas Allwood had a framing business in the Bloomsbury neighborhood of London between 1772 and 1793. His records note that he fabricated two frames for paintings by the famous artist George Stubbs in 1785 for Sir John Nelthorpe. For more information on Stubbs, see the sidebar on page 114. "Very few Stubbs paintings are in the original frame," Jimmie adds.

When choosing a frame, Jimmie advises, "Follow the form and color of the painting. I like to use a concave frame to sweep your eye into the painting to capture you; you will get what the artist intended you to see."

Finally, when it comes time to hang the painting Jimmie says, "Use your eye. I like below eye level; it makes the room taller and gives a less crowded effect."

OPPOSITE, CLOCKWISE FROM TOP LEFT: Inside a shadow box, miniature bronzes depict a hunting scene with a lady riding sidesaddle flanked by two huntsmen and hounds underfoot. A hand-painted wine goblet is for toasting to a successful day at the racetrack. A pair of jockey bookends holds highly collectible vintage postcards, including "Little Phostint Journeys," hidden inside faux books. John Maloney (far right, accepting trophy, and below in a portrait painted by Anthony Wills, who also did the portrait of former Secretary of State Henry Kissinger) was a successful racehorse trainer, and his daughter Sharon has followed in his footsteps. Horseshoes off the Maloney family's show hunters are recycled as frames for cherished photos. The collection of fox masks and fox brush are from successful hunting trips and shopping excursions. FOLLOWING PAGES: Sharon Maloney has added to her family collection of art and antiques by traveling around the world in search of just the right pieces.

BIG MAN ON CAMPUS

Landscape architect Ben Page of Nashville, Tennessee, has created a functional Kentucky working horse facility with an ambiance that embraces the rich history of the region.

Ben worked with Robert Clay, owner of the spectacular 1,800-acre Three Chimneys Farm in Woodford County, to design the facility. Robert started with 100 acres in 1972 and meticulously expanded. He is also a well-known steward of the land in the Lexington area and a founder of the Bluegrass Conservancy, a nonprofit land trust devoted to preserving the integrity of this celebrated expanse.

Three Chimneys could easily have been named after one of the old buildings on the farm. Instead, the inspiration came from the home address of one of Robert's friends from the College of William and Mary—Three Chimneys, St. George's, Bermuda.

Robert and his wife, Blythe, began their methodical renovation with a four-bedroom 1830s Greek Revival brick house on the farm that happened to have three chimneys. It was a bottom-to-top project. They had the painted black floors stripped, raised the roof to add more space, and thoughtfully integrated a family room addition in the original style.

As the business of breeding and raising Thoroughbreds grew, they added more land in separate segments, including some parcels across the Old Frankfort Pike. This expansion has turned out to be a blessing, giving each division of the enterprise—stallions, broodmares, and yearlings—its own identity.

Three Chimneys is noted for its star-studded cast of stallions. Among the grandest was Seattle Slew, the 1977 Triple Crown winner, who died in 2002. During his career at Three Chimneys, he sired more than a hundred stakes winners with combined earnings of $79 million. For each date with a broodmare, Seattle Slew commanded a fee of $300,000.

The stallion division includes many other illustrious names: Dynaformer (sire of 2006 Kentucky Derby winner Barbaro), Point Given, and 2004 Kentucky Derby and Preakness winner Smarty Jones.

"Robert called me to talk about the master plan at the farm," Ben recalls. "The first time we met in the log cabin office, there was a fire going in the fireplace and it felt like home. We talked, and I was blown away by the extraordinary things going on there and with the concept and the magnitude."

The objective was to sensitively expand, yet keep the intimate feeling of the farm, and Ben immediately had the answer. "Instead of a monolithic setting, we'd create a campus like Jefferson did at the University of Virginia. That was his vision of a village, and the same idea would hold true here."

A Kentucky native, Ben designed an equine village anchored by the log cabin office, taking the famous Lawn at Mr. Jefferson's university in Charlottesville as inspiration. "The history of Kentucky is rooted in the log cabin," he says. "It evokes *comfortable*."

Ben turned to Vic Hood of Franklin, Tennessee,

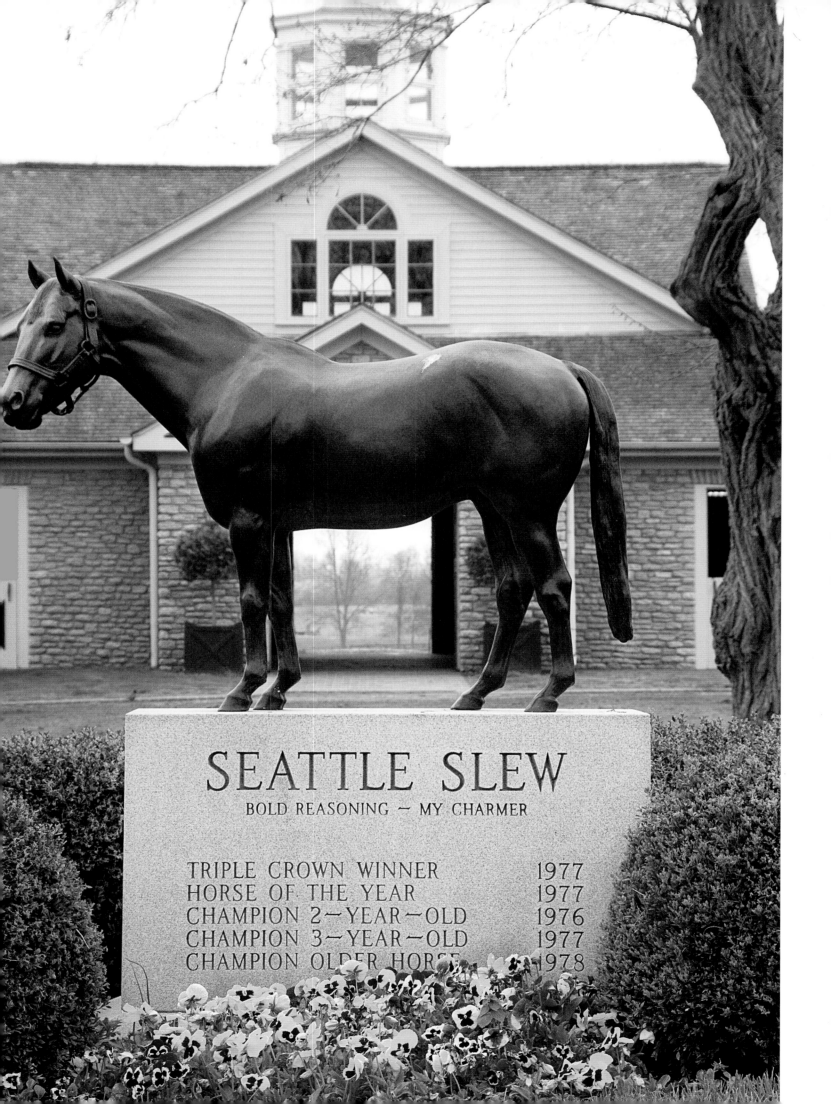

SEATTLE SLEW

BOLD REASONING ~ MY CHARMER

TRIPLE CROWN WINNER	1977
HORSE OF THE YEAR	1977
CHAMPION 2~YEAR~OLD	1976
CHAMPION 3~YEAR~OLD	1977
CHAMPION OLDER HORSE	1978

whose business, Leatherwood, stockpiles antique logs and structural elements. "We wanted all the buildings to have a strong architectural identity," Ben says. "We expanded the log cabin office just the way they used to do as the family grew." The extension is in an *L* shape. The length of the logs dictates the size of the room, which was known as a *crib*. Sometimes it's 12 by 12 and sometimes it's 14 by 16.

"The double crib log cabins still dot the landscape of Kentucky," adds Ben, who designs the buildings and then has a local architect do the drawings. "Many had a dog trot [passageway] in between; the center hall evolved from this. With the addition, we were able to add four more offices."

The offices were nearing completion just as a mighty wind of near tornado force ripped through the property, tearing up old oaks, tulip poplars, and ash trees. One of the oaks fell perilously close to the building, but fortunately missed. Ben brought in an arborist to clean up and stabilize the trees that could be saved.

"Then we replicated whatever had been there. We replaced an old bur oak with a young bur oak. We attempted to restore the integrity of the trees with a

CLOCKWISE FROM TOP RIGHT: Landscape architect Ben Jones wanted all the buildings to have a strong architectural identity. Leather halters actually worn by some of the famous horses at Three Chimneys line the office walls. The latest big man on campus, Smarty Jones. Robert Clay has thoughtfully added to the offices through the years. The collection of hand-painted snuff bottles were a gift from a Japanese client. Pale natural colors of wheat and hay were used on the office walls, with accent tables in bleached pine and a coordinating soft leather sofa.

diverse cross section." Ben integrated Kentucky coffee trees. He also added ginkgo trees, which transform from a vivid green into a glowing yellow, "for fall color." Dogwood, redbud, and silver bell trees were incorporated for a show of color from one season to the next.

Inside the offices, visitors gather in a central expanse at a seating area with bleached pine chairs covered in denim blue fabric. A library of reference magazines with pedigrees and racing records can be accessed by any staff member or client. The wall behind a desk in one office boasts the leather halters of some of Three Chimneys' most famous horses, a decorating touch often seen at many of the larger stud farms in Kentucky.

"These halters were actually worn by these stallions," a staff member explains. "These are not like the flags at the Capitol that are strung up the pole for three seconds."

The stallions are turned out in large paddocks following their morning engagements. They walk along paths between grass lawns, just as a college student walks to classes on campus. The same atmosphere spills over to the barns, where Ben says his designs are "all predicated on the axis relationship." As a visitor walks onto the lawn, or quad, the memorial statue of Seattle Slew by Julie Ware is visible, intentionally aligned with the center of the stud barn. A closer assessment reveals that the buildings have an asymmetric articulation. "The left side of the barn has more building to it than the right," Ben says. This was done to incorporate a view to an old allée of locust trees directly beyond on the same axis.

The log cabin vernacular continues with the barns around the expanse of lawn. The rough ashlar stone foundation was laid in horizontal lines, and the logs were hewed with half-dovetailed joints.

These architectural and landscape details, along with the honor roll of stallions, entice guests from around the world. Even Queen Elizabeth managed to build a stop here into her busy schedule on a visit to the United States in 2007. It was the third time she had been to the farm. But like many others, she just had to come to see the big man on campus . . . Smarty Jones.

Part III: At the Track

A BUGLER IN AN IMPRESSIVE

red jacket steps onto the racetrack to sound the familiar notes of the "Call to Post." Brilliant chestnut and gleaming bay horses parade past the grandstand, their jockeys wearing a spectrum of dazzling silks. The horses ease into the starting gate, jockeys barking last-minute warnings an instant before the gate crashes open. For centuries, jewelers, designers, and sporting artists have drawn inspiration from the legend and lure of the sport of kings.

Just like the bugle call on the racetrack, the horn could be heard in days gone by when coaches were the only form of wheeled transportation. Using a 3-foot-long copper or silver horn, which creates a strong, low-pitched tone, the guard riding on the back of the carriage would alert other coaches to his presence on the road. The calls include Change Horses, Near Side, Slacken Pace, Pull Up, and Steady. The notes were universal and remain in use today, as do many of the original carriage houses that once held the polished vehicles.

And when the silver racing trophies are proudly displayed on the mantel, they too require a bit of spit and polish before they shine as brightly as the horses and carriages.

PREVIOUS PAGES: *The Paddock at Keeneland* by artist Joanne Mehl. OPPOSITE, CLOCKWISE FROM TOP LEFT: Racing holds an allure, from the winner's circle to the early-morning rituals. Steeplechase jockey Danielle Hodsdon (far right, center). Many carriage houses in Saratoga have been renovated. There is a rich heritage of horses and music in Saratoga. The stables at Live Oak Stud in Ocala, Florida.

<104>

STUBBS AND WEBER

The early-morning traffic on Route 40 in Ocala, Florida, grinds along the east-west corridor. In an area where 29,000 residents are employed in the Thoroughbred business, there's a bumper-to-bumper procession of cars, tractor trailers, and pickups. To a visitor, the horse country of Marion County seems a mystery in the predawn darkness, particularly when trying to locate the proper entrance among a half-dozen options at Live Oak Stud.

The daily rhythm at the 4,500-acre farm commences at sunrise. Trainer Johnny Collins, wearing a red racing helmet and a red jacket to ward off the morning chill, emerges from the training barn. He oversees one hundred two-year-olds from atop a brown-and-white lead pony named Sunday Dinner. The young racehorses are systematically walked to the training track in sets of three for a jog or a light gallop. They are wearing red-and-white saddlecloths, and some have red leg wraps. Later in the day, they will eat oats from red buckets. All the exercise riders also sport red helmets.

Half of these two-year-olds are owned by Live Oak, which in turn is owned by Campbell's Soup heiress Charlotte Colket Weber, whose grandfather John T. Dorrance perfected the technique of condensing soup. In 1968, she purchased 1,000 acres from Peter Widener III, and over the years kept adding more land.

Live Oak has produced or raced Seeking Slew, High Fly, My Typhoon, and 2006 Eclipse champion Miesque's Approval. In 2005, the farm's racehorses earned $4.3 million from purses. The horses run in the farm's signature red-and-white polka-dot silks with black sleeves. The same polka dots appear on everything from the medicine cabinets in the yearling barn to the cocktail napkins, matches, and glassware in the main house.

The farm is organized by divisions—broodmare, stallion, yearling, and combined driving. Chester Weber, a son of Charlotte Weber, is a multiple national and international champion in the sport of combined driving with pairs and was the 2001–2002 reserve champion in the World Cup competition for four-in-hand drivers.

He trains his horses at Live Oak, where he lives with his Swedish-born wife, My Larsson, a jumper rider. Together they produce the Live Oak International Combined Driving Event, held in early March on the farm. Drivers and spectators from around the world flock to Live Oak to experience top-level international competition. With azaleas bursting in shades of pink and white, the enchanting springtime setting could make the groundskeepers at Augusta National envious, and the ancient live oak trees, dripping with Spanish moss, add tranquil definition to the landscape.

As the workday at Live Oak concludes, Chester and My wrap up their duties in the barns and head inside to prepare dinner or for an evening out with friends. The sun begins to dip in the west as cars and pickup trucks pull out the gates to head home. There are seventy-five employees, including gardeners, maintenance crew, riders, grooms, and office staff.

LIVE OAK STUD

The economic impact of the Thoroughbred business in Florida exceeds $1 billion annually. Thoroughbred auctions are held several times a year at the Ocala Breeder's Sales Complex, where potential champions sell for thousands of dollars. However, not all of the drivers in the evening rush hour toil in the horse business. More than twenty-four thousand calves are born each year in Marion County, which boasts of one of the largest chapters in the Florida Cattlemen's Association. The Ocala Bull Sale, established in 1946, is the oldest such event in the United States. In addition to a string of award-winning Thoroughbreds, the Webers' Live Oak Plantation has a cattle division with eight hundred Charolais, Angus, and Brahman cows.

LEFT, FROM TOP: Chester Weber drove his family's Clydesdales as a little boy and now operates the combined driving division at Live Oak. Sculptor John Skeaping's draft horse. Trainer Johnny Collins watches the morning workouts from atop Sunday Dinner. OPPOSITE: A rug beneath the trophy collection is a reminder of the family's connection to Campbell's soup.

OPPOSITE: Chester Weber's trophies include five national championships. LEFT, FROM TOP: More than a hundred two-year-olds are in training at Live Oak. Miniature bronzes adorn the mantel: *Hunting the Stag,* by British sporting artist John Nost Sartorius (1759–1828), hangs above. Live Oak's familiar red polka dot silks can be spotted everywhere. BELOW: The red and black theme even extends to the feed tubs.

MASTER OF ART

The collections at Live Oak are as mesmerizing as the horses. Chester's trophies are displayed in a bookcase in his office along with family photos in silver frames. There are several small jeweled replicas of the iconic Campbell's tomato soup can, an homage to the family business.

A version of the painting *A Grey Hunter with a Groom and a Greyhound at Creswell Crags,* by George Stubbs, a treasured item in the world of equestrian art, hangs in one of the rooms at Live Oak.

Stubbs, born in Liverpool, England, in August 1724, is best known for his paintings of horses and is revered by connoisseurs of British equestrian art. When he was twenty, Stubbs began a six-year study of human anatomy at York Hospital in England. His illustrations were included in an 1851 publication, "Essay Toward a Complete New System of Midwifery," by John Burton. Stubbs was captivated by anatomy, and this fascination played into his subsequent illustrations. During the 1750s, he spent a year and a half dissecting horses while living in the countryside in Lincolnshire. *The Anatomy of the Horse* was published with his engravings as a folio in 1766 and is a coveted item among collectors. The large drawings brought Stubbs fame throughout Europe. The originals of this collection are now at the Royal Academy in London.

Stubbs's highly accurate and meticulous work drew the admiration of the aristocracy of Britain, including the Marquis of Rockingham, who in 1762 commissioned Stubbs to paint King George III on his horse Whistlejacket. Upon viewing the 97-by-115-inch painting of the spirited horse without the rider, the Marquis took it as it was.

"He loved it," says Louisa Woodville, an adjunct professor of art history at George Mason University. "He thought anything else in the way of landscape or rider would rob it of the compelling power it had at that stage."

The masterpiece now resides in the collection of the National Gallery in London. The Prince of Wales of Stubbs's time (the future King George IV) also was a patron. The painting he commissioned, *The Prince of Wales's Phaeton, with the Coachman Samuel Thomas*

and a Tiger-Boy, is dated 1793 and is part of the Royal Collection of Her Majesty Queen Elizabeth II.

Stubbs settled into a home at 22 Somerset Street in the Marylebone section of London and continued to receive commissions. He painted in enamel on earthenware pieces produced by Josiah Wedgwood and had high hopes for this innovation. But it was poorly received, with reviews at the time referring to the technique as a disgrace. Clearly, it did not enhance his reputation.

One thing that did increase esteem for Stubbs was the paintings he did of exotic animals: cheetahs, lions, monkeys, giraffes, and rhinoceroses. Prints and posters of his African zebra set in English woodland, now at the Yale Center for British Art in New Haven, Connecticut, are included in the décor of many equestrian homes.

Stubbs died in July 1806, and only three exhibitions of his work were held between his death and 1914. Major museums did not begin to seek out his paintings until just after the turn of the twentieth century. Now his paintings hang in some of the best museums in the world, including the Tate in London, the National Gallery of Scotland in Edinburgh, the Walker Art Gallery in Liverpool, and the National Gallery of Art in Washington, D.C. Much of Stubbs's popularity can be attributed to the efforts of the late Paul Mellon, a generous philanthropist, art connoisseur, anglophile, and horse lover. Mellon was the patron saint of the Paul Mellon Centre for Studies in British Art in London and the Yale Center for British Art, which holds many pieces of Stubbs's work and is the largest and most comprehensive collection of British art outside the United Kingdom.

The privilege of owning a Stubbs horse painting today would cost a collector several million dollars.

A similar adaptation of the painting at Live Oak can be found at the Tate in London. According to Louisa Woodville, "Stubbs would frequently have a formula for portraying horses that he would turn to again and again." Admirers of his paintings are more than willing to look at them all again and again.

SHINING BRIGHTLY

Man o' War received the usual welcome as he came out on parade, this time accompanied by a lead pony. It would seem that Man o' War fully realizes his own importance in the racing world, for on parade he is at his very best, always high-spirited and gifted with all the attributes of a real show animal.

—Fred Van Ness, *New York Times*, August 13, 1919

The larger-than-life bronze figure of Man o' War now at the Kentucky Horse Park was designed by sculptor Herbert Haseltine while the horse was still alive. It took eight years to complete, and for anyone who has ever visited Lexington in the past sixty years, the image of this equine icon surely endures.

Haseltine, born in 1877 in Rome, lived in Italy until the age of fifteen. His parents were American and his father, William Stanley Haseltine, was a respected landscape painter. In the genre of sculpture, Herbert Haseltine became the Rodin of equine art. His clients included British statesman Winston Churchill and artist John Singer Sargent. His work is represented in the collections of Queen Elizabeth; the Smithsonian Museum of American Art in Washington, D.C.; and the National Museum of Racing and Hall of Fame in Saratoga Springs, New York.

Sportsman Marshall Field commissioned Haseltine to execute a series of twenty-six British champion animals. The group was first held by the Field Museum in Chicago and later purchased by Paul Mellon and given to the Virginia Museum of Fine Arts in Richmond, Virginia. A pair of Indian horse's heads, cast in 24-carat gold and embellished with diamonds, rubies, pearls, sapphires, emeralds, and jade, was commissioned by heiress Barbara Hutton.

In Washington, admirers of Haseltine's work can see an equestrian statue of British Field Marshal Sir John Dill at Arlington National Cemetery and a statue of George Washington at the National Cathedral. The latter was originally covered in gold gilt, which was later completely removed following vandalism.

The horse that George Washington is depicted riding was inspired by Man o' War. Horses enthralled Haseltine all his life. One in particular captured his imagination: the immense chestnut colt Man o' War. Born March 29, 1917, he was fondly known as Big Red. The 16.2-hand horse won twenty of twenty-one races, including the Preakness, the Belmont, and Travers Stakes. He was not entered in the Kentucky Derby, and his only loss was to the aptly named Upset in the Sanford Memorial before he was retired to stud in January 1921.

When Haseltine first saw Man o' War in 1934, the horse was shining brightly. Haseltine recalled him as a "golden chestnut, with metallic reflection accentuated when out in the sun."

Haseltine returned many times to Faraway Farm to work on the numerous phases that go into completing a sculpture of this magnitude. Occasionally the artist would bring a sack of apples to the big horse. He took hundreds of measurements "from the top of his ears down to his hoofs," and the massive stallion never budged when Haseltine bent under his belly. Visitors from all over came to visit the horse and watch Haseltine work. One woman gave him a fifty-cent tip. Another fan sent a letter addressed "Herbert Haseltine c/o Man o' War, Lexington," which was delivered promptly.

<117>

Herbert Haseltine
(British, 1877-1962)
'Suffolk Punch - MCMXXIX'

© HERBERT HASELTINE
MCMXLVI

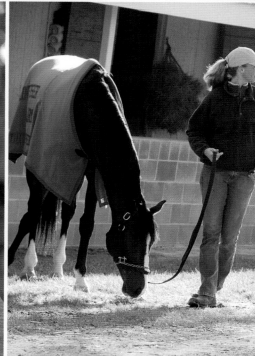

PREVIOUS PAGES: In life and in death, Man o' War has captured the hearts of many visitors in Lexington, Kentucky. Sculptor Herbert Haseltine (top center) spent eight years completing a larger-than-life bronze of the great horse; it now stands at the Kentucky Horse Park, which hosts many equestrian activities each year, including the Rolex Three-Day Event. Mr. and Mrs. Warren Wright Sr. (center) owned Calumet Farm, which began in 1924 with William Monroe Wright, founder of the baking powder business of the same name. Citation with Eddie Arcaro (bottom center) captured the 1948 Triple Crown for Calumet Farm. RIGHT: The racehorse business begins before dawn in Kentucky.

The firm of Rochette and Parzini, which also made the altar at St. Patrick's Cathedral in Manhattan, did the casting. The first casting was unacceptable to Haseltine; it was full of holes because scrap metal was used due to a wartime shortage. The casting was done over twice more, and Haseltine hired artist Joseph Ternbach to do the final touches, called *chasing.*

Man o' War's faithful groom, Will Harbut, passed away in October 1947. The horse died of a broken heart twenty-nine days later, on November 1, and it is believed he was the first horse ever embalmed. He was buried at Faraway Farm in an oak casket lined with his silk racing colors of black and yellow. Thousands attended the funeral, which was broadcast on the radio and filmed for newsreels. Haseltine's bronze was unveiled on October 16, 1948. In 1977, the grave and statue were moved to the Kentucky Horse Park, where the towering figure of Man o' War continues to shine brightly.

Also located at the Kentucky Horse Park, the 524-piece Calumet Farm Trophy Collection of gold and silver urns, cups, trays, pitchers, platters, bowls, tureens, and julep cups sparkles inside the custom-made cases designed to replicate those at the farm. The Calumet Collection is on display thanks to the devoted Save the Calumet Trophies committee, led by longtime Calumet Farm secretary Margaret B. Glass and James E. "Ted" Bassett III, then president and now a trustee of the Keeneland Association.

ABOVE: At the Kentucky Horse Park, visitors will see a parade of breeds, the International Museum of the Horse, the American Saddlebred Museum, and a host of retired equine champions. BELOW: Trophies from the Calumet Farm collection include two Triple Crown titles, eight Kentucky Derby victories, and seven Preakness wins.

Horses raised at Calumet form a parade of some of the most recognizable names in racing history—Whirlaway, Citation, Tim Tam, Forward Pass, and Alydar. They have won two Triple Crown titles, eight Kentucky Derbys, and seven Preaknesses.

Following a financial downturn, the 770-acre farm was auctioned and sold in 1992. The trophies were in danger of being sold off piece by piece to pay remaining debts. The Save the Calumet Trophies committee raised $1.2 million with 1,189 donations from all fifty states and four foreign countries. The commonwealth of Kentucky contributed an additional $1.5 million, for a total of $2.7 million. But it wasn't until September 4, 1998, after an exhausting battle with creditors and other legal problems, that the collection officially earned a lifelong home.

The trophies now glow thanks to a team of volunteers, who come in for so-called Silver Saturdays to polish the Calumet Collection. For people wanting information on the best method for caring for silver, Don Williams, the senior conservator at the Smithsonian Museum Conservation Institute in Washington, D.C., has good news. "Silver is not harmed by light and normal ranges of heat," he says, adding that the main problem is pollution. "The oxides, chlorides, and sulfites in the atmosphere cause damage." For example, it's important not to display silver near a hot tub or a swimming pool, both of which emit chloride.

White cotton gloves should be worn when handling silver. The process of caring for silver on display, such as trophies, requires three steps: cleaning, polishing, and coating.

In his book, *Saving Stuff,* Don discourages the use of over-the-counter silver polishes. "Coarse abrasives get the tarnish off in a hurry, but they take off the silver, too," he writes. Instead, he suggests preparing a cleaning solution of equal parts acetone and alcohol and putting the mixture in a squirt bottle. While wearing an organic solvent mask and paint-stripping gloves, use a soft brush to clean all the surfaces. "Then, use a flannel cloth to dry the silver," he says.

For the next step, use Don's favorite formula, which can be made by mixing 1 teaspoon ultrafine polishing abrasive (pulverized limestone, also known as *powdered chalk*) from the garden supply or hardware store or whiting from an art supply store with 1 tablespoon alcohol or mineral spirits. "It's best to apply the formula with a lint-free cloth and rub carefully," he says. When the silver is shining brightly, use the cleaning solution to take off any remaining bits of the slurry. Dry with the cloth. The final touch is an application of Krylon acrylic spray lacquer. "It's not permanent," Don says, "but you won't have to polish again until it wears off, which is usually a couple of years."

ABOVE: Spindletop Hall, now a private club for University of Kentucky alumni and friends, was formerly owned by Texas oil heiress Pansy Yount, and many of her trophies remain here. When Pansy Yount was still in residence, the servants were not allowed to take more than $10,000 worth of silver out of the case at one time in order to polish it. OPPOSITE: At the Kentucky Horse Park, volunteers come in for Silver Saturdays to polish all the trophies.

DESIGNING THE KENTUCKY DERBY TROPHY

The Kentucky Derby began in 1854 and is the most coveted victory in horse racing. The first trophy was bestowed in 1922, in the form of a six-piece gold buffet service awarded to Ben Block, owner of the winning horse, Moorish.

The first version of a permanent award known as the Kentucky Derby Gold Cup was presented at the fiftieth anniversary of the race to Rosa Hoots, owner of the 1924 winner Black Gold. It was designed by George Lewis Graff of Lemon and Sons in Louisville, where the race takes place the first Saturday in May at Churchill Downs racetrack.

Twenty-two inches tall and made of solid gold, the trophy is created by hand over a period of three months from a 14-carat gold brick and enhanced with 18-carat gold segments of a horse and rider and horseshoe handles. It weighs 56 ounces, including the jade base. For the 75th Derby in 1949, the 100th Derby in 1974, and the 125th Derby in 1999, the trophy was accented with emeralds and diamonds.

In 1975, the New England Sterling Company of North Attleboro, Massachusetts, took over making the trophy. In 1999, a minor change was made to put the horseshoe on the front facing up, symbolizing good luck in the frequently superstitious horse world. (When a horseshoe is facing down, all the luck can spill out.)

If a Kentucky Derby trophy were to be sold on the public market, its estimated value would range from $60,000 to $100,000, depending on fluctuating gold prices and the popularity of the winning horse. And yes, the owners do get to keep a replica of the trophy.

" The Save the Calumet Trophies committee raised $1.2 million with 1,189 donations from fifty states and four foreign countries. The commonwealth of Kentucky put in an additional $1.5 million, for a total of $2.7 million. On September 4, 1998, after an exhausting battle with creditors and various other legal issues, the collection officially had a lifelong home at the Kentucky Horse Park. It is now appraised at $3.5 million. "

EQUINE ARTISTS

A powerful painting draws in the observer with compelling composition and captures the light in an enthralling moment frozen for generations to follow. Knowing and understanding the subject is the key to success for all artists; for those specializing in equine art, there is also a living and breathing four-legged factor.

Artist Andre Pater was commissioned to do a series of paintings of Smarty Jones, the 2004 Kentucky Derby winner, as the horse entered Three Chimneys Farm to stand at stud in Kentucky. When Andre first laid eyes on the liver chestnut, he says, "He looked like an average horse. However, upon closer examination he had tremendous quality of conformation."

Andre decided to portray the horse in three key moments of racing: going to the track to race, crossing the finish line in a flush of victory, and coming back around the track after the race. "The horse has his head down and is relaxed as they return after the race, and the jockey is up on his legs in the stirrups," he says in his charming Polish accent.

As a young boy, Andre traveled to the countryside of his native land on summer breaks with his family. "I'd do anything to be around horses," he recalls. "I liked to feed them. I loved the smell. The fact that I'm a painter goes back to my fascination with their movement and power."

Andre's ability to capture the horse's intricate actions in pastels and oils has led to sold-out shows around the world. "He studied the classical methods at the Kraków Academy

of Fine Arts and learned to draw," says Greg Ladd, who represents Andre at the Cross Gate Gallery in Lexington.

Susan Van Wagoner, an artist based in Middleburg, Virginia, believes that capturing details is vital for her life-size works in pastel, colored pencil, and oil on linen. Long before she begins a portrait, she spends hours watching her subjects roam in a field or roll in a paddock to catch their particular quirks.

"Horses have different personalities, which come out when they work, play, interact with other horses—even shake after a swim," she says. "Everything they do brings out their individual traits, and I like to watch them to discover their personalities as well as their physical characteristics."

Susan's painting of the pony Rosmel's Caprisun rolling in the dirt shows how her observations enhance her art. She usually works on commission, so once a horse owner has hired her to do a portrait, she spends hours getting to know her subject, often flying around the country to get more intimate views.

"This is a very fancy show pony. I took all kinds of photos of her from every direction," Susan recalls of her visit to Charlottesville to see Rosmel's Caprisun. "She has a pretty head and a beautiful tail. I watched her trot on the line, and after her workout she was turned out in the paddock and she lay down to roll."

Susan did several preliminary sketches for owner Mary Elizabeth Moore, one a head study with the bridle and one of the horse standing. Almost as an afterthought,

<127>

she included a rolling-in-the-dirt sketch. "She loved that one," Susan says. "Horses don't just perform in the horse show; they like to play, too."

Once back in her third-floor studio after her series of observations, Susan always begins by painting the eyes of the horse. "They come alive," she says. "That's just how I see things, as they are. So when I draw, I know them so well, I know the direction of the hair."

Enrique Castro learned about horses while growing up in the countryside of Argentina. He started to draw professionally at age thirteen and later bred polo ponies and managed a racing stud farm.

Then Enrique went to work at a gallery in London and stayed twenty years while perfecting his oil-on-paper technique. Jeanne Chisholm, of Chisholm Gallery in Pine Plains, New York, represents Enrique: "He knows the sport of polo intimately, and he's captured the swift athleticism and relationship of pony and rider with enviable accuracy in his work *Offside Forehand,*" she relates.

French artist Frédérique Lavergne, who paints magnificent dressage horses, says, "I was born into a world inhabited by horses. I was in permanent contact with horses during my childhood."

Frédérique studied philosophy, communication, graphic arts, and illustration and began working in the artistic/bohemian section of Montparnasse in Paris. A turn in her personal life led her to abandon the city a few years ago and move to the southwest of France, close to Spain. "I found great happiness to have my first horse, Hiram," she says. In addition to the pleasure of riding he gave her, Hiram also inspired Frédérique's painting and sculpture.

"At the time of a tour in Andalusia, I discovered the Andalusian and Lusitanian horses. Their aesthetic and exceptional expressivity touched me," she says. "Breeders, artists of the equestrian spectacle, entrust their horses like models to me. I work to transmit the emotions resulting from the meetings with their horses."

PREVIOUS PAGES, LEFT: Artist Andre Pater captured jockey Stewart Elliott's victory salute as he and Smarty Jones won the 2004 Kentucky Derby. ABOVE: French artist Frédérique Lavergne, who painted this work, studied philosophy, communication, graphic arts, and illustration. OPPOSITE, ABOVE: Juli Kirk's artwork was part of a Masters of Foxhounds Association traveling exhibition. OPPOSITE, BELOW: Susan Van Wagoner's study of the pony Rosmel's Caprisun rolling in the paddock.

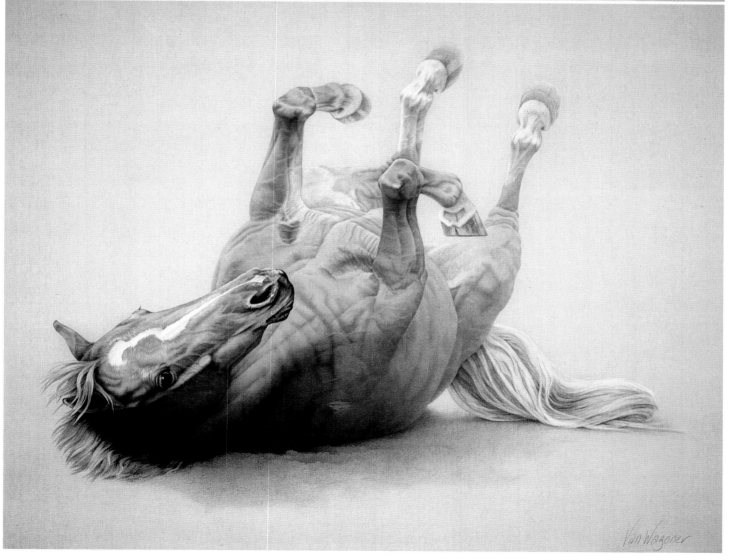

Acadian Four

Kathi Peters approachs equine art from a different angle. While other artists work on large canvases, Kathi's efforts are intricate and detailed.

"The paper cuts are all done from one piece of paper, cut by hand," Kathi explains. "A slip of the knife can mean a whip goes missing or a horse's leg disappears."

"*Acadia Four* is an image of the coaching crowd that came up to Acadia late each summer for a week of partying and driving on Rockefeller's marvelous carriage roads in Acadia National Park on Mount Desert Island," says Kathi, who works in a studio, Cob Cottage, in Morrill, Maine.

There are several other genuine equine artists who may or may not put a lot of thought into their work, and Smarty Jones is one of them. In an appropriately named program called Moneigh, famous racehorses are given a paintbrush and paints. (Smarty used his nose and signed his work with a hoofprint.) Their paintings are then auctioned on eBay to raise money for the Thoroughbred adoption organization, ReRun, in Helmetta, New Jersey.

For any piece of art that is going to take up a special and permanent place on the wall, the owners needs to learn about the artist and then bond with the subject matter. "Study the painting," says Greg Ladd. "A person's eye is usually drawn to something that is appealing."

"You create a relationship with the painting you are going to live with; it becomes a quintessential part of your space. The energy of a painting can bring harmony to a person's life," says Jeanne Chisholm.

OPPOSITE, CLOCKWISE FROM TOP: Kathi Peters's paper cut *Acadian Four*. Artist Enrique Castro learned about horses while growing up in Argentina. HRH Prince Khalid bin Abdullah commissioned Hazel Morgan's study of mares and foals at his Juddmonte Farm. Michael Ponce's oil on panel *Harvard vs. Yale*. RIGHT, FROM TOP: During the yearling sales in Saratoga, the Cross Gate Gallery mounts a show of sporting art. Evelyn Cowles's painting *Start with the Hoof*. Smarty Jones is also a talented artist. Live Oak's *My Typhoon,* by Robert Clark. *Saratoga Sunlight,* by Christine Cancelli. FOLLOWING PAGES: Inside the Chisholm Gallery in Pine Plains, New York.

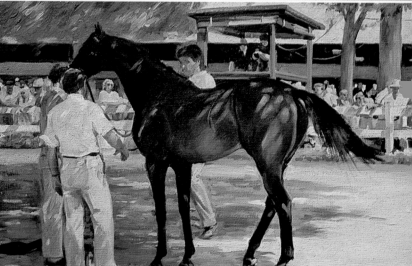

FORGING AHEAD

Several blocks from the bustling commercial thoroughfare of Dixie Highway in West Palm Beach, Florida, a nondescript building in the middle of an industrial complex houses a foundry where artist Beverly Zimmer produces exquisite pieces of equine sculpture.

Meanwhile, on the east side of the nearby Intracoastal Waterway, the winter social swirl is in full swing in Palm Beach. The midafternoon sun glares off the gleaming windows along Worth Avenue, the posh town's über-chic three-block retail strip. At the fashionable Worth Avenue bistro Taboo, stylishly dressed local women meet for high-priced, low-carb lunches, and whispering lovers rendezvous over minty mojitos.

As visitors step out of Taboo and cross the street, they soon pass number 224A, home of the Gallery Biba. A majestic pair of life-size bronze horse busts in a dark finish of liver of sulfur and a white patina called bismuth dominates the stark white space.

At the height of one recent season, gallery owner Biba St. Croix hosted a lavish opening. That night, Beverly Zimmer shed her work clothes for a long black velvet gown. Her black-and-white horse sculptures, titled *Curious* and *Question,* were making their debut, at $70,000 for the pair. For Beverly, the precious pieces marked the culmination of six months of grueling work. But her path to this glamorous Worth Avenue opening actually began when she was a horse-crazy little girl growing up in Willow Grove, Pennsylvania.

"I had girlfriends in school who had their own horses, so I'd draw pictures of them and my friends would pay me twenty dollars a pop," she recalls. "That bought two riding lessons."

Beverly expanded her entrepreneurial art skills to remodeling plastic models of horses. It turned out that slightly altering or repositioning the popular Breyer horse figures was a booming industry.

"I was a nut. I did anything to make money," Beverly says. "That's how I got my start. It's empowering when a teenager gets three hundred fifty dollars. I bought a top-of-the-line riding saddle; it was great."

Remodeling horse figures struck a chord with the aspiring artist, who says she has always been able to visualize her work in three dimensions. While attending Tyler Art School in Philadelphia, she took a job riding horses and working in the stables to finance tuition payments. "I did everything that goes along with it, including shoveling, feeding, and cleaning tack," she says.

As Beverly commuted from the barns to the classroom, she was frequently disheveled in battered boots and grubby jeans, but fit right in because "it was art school, so you never had to look good." Several times she brought a horse to school for her fellow students to study for sculpture classes.

"The teachers didn't want to see pretty horses," she says. "They wanted us to go beyond traditional art. They pushed me to explore why I was obsessed. I studied the core of the horse and the locomotive and skeletal system. It was nice to experiment as a student, and now my sculpture has a whirlwind feel, a horsiness and depth."

Her work is displayed in a wide variety of settings. An 18-foot-long series of horses was commissioned by one of the founders of the Palm Beach Equine Clinic and can be seen in its lobby. Barbara Stegen ordered a 41-inch-high bronze entitled *Let's Dance,* depicting her daughter Tara's favorite horse. Beverly's work is displayed in living rooms, gardens, and even on the entry posts of one Palm Beach mansion whose owner prefers not to be named.

Forge Hill Sculpture, her business, has also allowed her to own a home in the horse community of Aiken, South Carolina. In the winter, Beverly travels to Florida with her mare, Carly.

"I was one of those kids," she says. "From the time I was six years old, there was no question I was going to be an artist."

FROM TWEED TO TULLE

Worn on daytime tweeds or on evening tulle ball gowns, classic equestrian-style jewelry combines the traditional images of fox, hound, and horse in an unassuming way. Bracelets, pins, and rings inspired by pieces of tack such as bridle reins, boots, and the ever-popular snaffle bit can be spotted at horse races and horse shows around the world.

Many of the designs are in gold and silver, and some are even set with accents of diamonds or sapphires. Still, for this crowd, it's never been about the bling. It's all about timeless and tasteful, leaving the flash and glitz for someone else.

Popular pieces include colorful custom-designed enamels on belt buckles and earrings, reverse intaglio crystals in the form of brooches and rings, and one-of-a-kind hand-carved cameos.

BUCKLE UP

Equestrians Gregg and Linden Ryan have a hectic schedule. They start at dawn exercising horses before Gregg goes to the office, where he serves as the president of Lee & Mason Financial Services. Linden rides more horses before heading off to her work in real estate. When not working they can be found at the steeplechase races, where Gregg still competes as a leading amateur rider. Linden was a member of the American team that earned a bronze medal in the Three-Day Event competition at the 2000 Olympics in Sydney, Australia.

They are constantly traveling between homes in upstate New York and Virginia; to do so with ease they pack light, often changing from jeans to suits on the fly.

For the Ryans and many other horse people, jewelry must transition from the barn to a luncheon at the races to an early evening party. Designer Daniel Sigal's enamel jewelry is intended to suit no matter the occasion. Using a time-consuming ancient technique, he applies a series of colors to each piece of gold, silver, or copper. After each color is applied, the piece is fired in a kiln at temperatures of 1300° to 1500°F. Examples of this craft can be seen in museums on historic bibelots from Greece and Rome, and Daniel's technique is similar to that of the well-known Russian artist Peter Carl Fabergé—creator of those priceless jeweled eggs.

Daniel's work consists of items such as a small pair of earrings or cuff links with a fox motif or a belt buckle embossed with the owner's racing silks. "I mix the colors optically as you see light going through stained glass," says Daniel, an architect who transitioned his design talents into his current career twenty years ago. The colors transform with each application and firing, with "only the slightest variation in color from the previous step." The firing time for each stage is one to four minutes, and each piece is fired between 120 and 150 times.

"I use vitreous powder colors, also called *jewelry enamel*," says Daniel, who works from his studio in Lexington, Kentucky. The transparent, translucent, or opaque powders are infused with minerals such as cobalt, which produces a brilliant blue. "I apply in many fashions depending on the desired end result, by using a brush, a knife, or a sieve."

<137>

SPORTING GLASS

Reverse intaglio crystals are known simply as *crystals* in the horse world. Made from a cabochon (half-round) crystal, they come in round, oval, rectangular, and sometimes triangular shapes. The underside of the crystal is etched in reverse with intricate sporting scenes or animals and then delicately painted. Some of the brushes used have just one or two fine hairs.

Once finished, the back of the crystal is covered with mother-of-pearl and encased in gold. When seen from the front, the rings, earrings, pendants, and brooches have an exquisite three-dimensional depth of field.

Crystals were first made in the mid-1800s, and, according to Duncan Semmens, director at Hancocks & Co. Jewellers Ltd. in London, the Belgian-born artist Émile Marius Pradier's work is the most sought-after. "His work can be identified by the thorn," Duncan says. "He incorporated a carved thorn into the crystal with all types of birds and other animals." Duncan also cites the circa 1850s work of British artists Thomas Cooke and Thomas Bean.

"I first became interested in selling crystals in the 1970s," says Marion Maggiolo, owner of Horse Country in Warrenton, Virginia. She praises the work of the late Helmet Busmer from Germany. "[His crystals] aren't too showy, and they look good with sporting clothes."

Ginny Howard of Lexington, Kentucky, sells antique crystals and recommends seeking the work of one of the original British craftsmen. "His last name was Essex, and he signed his pieces. They're very hard to find but are still around. He also did enamelware," Ginny says. "I know people who'd rather own a big crystal than diamonds. They love the art that goes into it. Horse people are sporting people, and these pieces reflect their interest."

UNDER THE SEA

Thirty-something Massino Falanga of Torre del Greco, Italy, carves one-of-a-kind cameos for Mystique Jewelers in Virginia. "I think of a cameo as a very classic piece

that you'd see women in England wear years ago. It's a relic from back in time, a moment and a memory," says store owner Liz Miller.

Each stunning cameo is hand-carved from shells imported from the Bahamas. With a diamond wheel, the shell is cut into pieces from the bottom or helmet section (known in Italy as the *prima coppa*). The shape of the cameo—round, oval, or rectangular—follows.

Massino carves the cameos with a knife-like instrument called a *bulino*. Many of his pieces portray horses as powerful figures in a delicate, timeless setting, including his stunning image of three horses surrounded by 18-carat gold and freshwater pearls.

Just one concluding fashion tip: All the unwritten rules of simple and refined equestrian-inspired jewelry fly out the window when it comes to Mother's three strands of 10-millimeter pearls or Grandmother's emeralds and diamonds. After all, no one ever said they couldn't be worn with a tweed jacket at the steeplechase races or with a beautiful tulle gown at the hunt ball.

ABOVE: These bangles from Live It Jewelry, designed by Sheri Mount, were inspired by the polo matches in Wellington, Florida. CLOCKWISE FROM TOP LEFT: Tiny snaffle bits and buckles hold these golden horseshoes in place. An enamel fox clasp anchors a pink polo tie. Olympic equestrian Linden Ryan wears these tasteful and understated earrings from dawn to dusk. A hand-carved equestrian-inspired cameo from Italy is surrounded by freshwater pearls. Reverse intaglio crystal jewelry is extremely popular with horse people. Daniel Sigal's enamel designs can be custom made in racing silk colors. Surrounded by moonstones and sapphires, this oval crystal would be perfect for the hunt ball.

SILKS AND SATINS

The inspired patterns on the colorful racing silks worn by jockeys date to October 1762, when the British Jockey Club introduced the concept to an elite group including seven dukes, four earls, two baronets, one marquis, one viscount, and one lord. The objective was to avoid confusion among spectators, and the owners themselves, in differentiating riders and horses.

"The stewards, therefore, hope . . . that the named gentlemen will take care that the riders be provided with dresses accordingly," the British Jockey Club announced at the time.

The Jockey Club of the United States was founded in 1894 and maintains offices in Lexington, Kentucky, and New York City, where owners register their respective colors. (Joint registration, as in Mr. and Mrs., is not allowed.) More than thirty thousand silks are on file, the oldest—John Morris's scarlet silks—dated 1894.

Registration specifications are precise. The front and back of the silks must be the same color. Two colors can be used on the body of the silks and two more colors on the sleeves, for a total of four. "You may have an acceptable emblem or up to three initials on the ball, yoke, circle, or braces design," Jockey Club rules state. "You may have one initial on the opposite shoulder of the sash design, the box frame, or the diamond."

Some of the shapes for the configuration on the silks include diagonal stripes, cross sashes, blocks, shamrocks, diamonds, and 3^1/$_2$-inch balls from right shoulder to left hip. For the sleeves, the Jockey Club registration forms include chevrons, two hoops, circles, diamond seams, halves, vertical halves, dots, and solids.

Eighty-something Patricia Headley Green's Lexington, Kentucky, business, Silks Unlimited, incorporates these designs onto racing silks for customers from all over the world. As a native of central Kentucky, Patricia has felt the impact of the horse business all her life. Her father, Hal Price Headley, was a founder of the Keeneland Association and racetrack and served as president from 1935 to 1951 (see the sidebar on page 146).

Patricia operates a cottage industry making racing silks from her shop on West Second Street. "I don't sew a stitch, but I have a good eye for color," she says. "So many men come in here and tell me what they want. They tell me lavender and pink and then when I show it to them, they say, 'Oh, that's purple and brown.' That's because so many men are color-blind."

Patricia reviews the designs with the owners and then makes a worksheet with fabric swatches, thread, and snaps attached. She has four workers who cut the fabric and then take it home to sew. "There are no sewing machines here," she points out. Given her client base of twenty-five hundred, Patricia says she has no need to advertise or even have her own website. Prices vary according to the complexity of the designs. She also makes custom-designed saddlecloths.

"The longer someone has been in the business of horse racing, the simpler the designs," Patricia says. "The older names in racing, Phipps and Hancock, are solid colors.

THE DARLEY TEST
81st RUNNING   6-5-06

SWAP FLIPAROO

OWNER: NOBEAU FARM
TRAINER: H. ALLEN JERKENS
JOCKEY: EIBAR COA

Heaven knows what [people] might want to put on them nowadays in the way of a logo. In the beginning, it was simple. There were some with a single sash and then the cross sash came along."

One of the most identifiable sets of silks in recent history is the royal blue and white blocks with blue-and-white-striped sleeves of Penny Tweedy Chenery's Meadow Stable, worn by Hall of Fame jockey Ron Turcotte on Secretariat while capturing the 1973 Triple Crown.

Sarah Marr uses these distinctive royal blue-and-white silks in her equestrian purse line, Episode 39. "In the early days of horse racing," Sarah explains, "the original purse holding the winner's money was, in fact, a silk drawstring purse that was hung up near the finish line and taken down after the race. It was called the take-down purse, then shortened to purse."

Sarah's designs have authentic horseshoes as the handles and have been spotted on the arms of former first lady of New York Libby Pataki, former first lady of Maryland Kendel Ehrlich, Debbie Finley of West Point Thoroughbreds, and leading owners and breeders Mildred Boyce of Kentucky, Theresa Behrendt of New York, and Charlotte Weber of Florida.

Proud owners also use their racing colors in decorating their homes—on everything from doormats to glasses to bathroom fixtures. Lawn jockeys bearing the owner's colors greet guests at farms and estates around the country.

These ornaments have a curious history. The original lawn jockeys depicted an African-American footman or groom holding a ring used as a hitching post or grasping a lantern. One folktale describes the statues as a tribute to twelve-year-old slave Tom "Jocko" Graves, who stood clutching a lantern on the banks of the Delaware River one frigid night in 1776 to light a path for General George Washington and his men.

During the Civil War, the statues were reported to indicate safe haven along the southern routes of the Underground Railroad if a green ribbon was tied to the arm. A red ribbon warned of danger. Over time, the lawn ornament evolved to a jockey, first with blackface, perhaps because there were so many African-American jockeys in the early 1900s. The politically incorrect and often offensive ornaments eventually faded to white.

Artist and graphic designer Kevin Titter paints custom racing silks colors on lawn jockeys. A man of multiple creative talents, he wrote and designed the book *Chesapeake City: The Canal Town Through the Years* and designs the layout for the *Steeplechase Times* and other horse-related publications based in Fair Hill, Maryland.

The 46-inch-high aluminum lawn jockey statues weigh 42 pounds. Kevin sands the rough edges, then

covers the statues with a primer coat before beginning to paint the custom colors. Once complete, the lawn jockey is taken to a body shop and covered with a clear coat of finish. The entire process takes about three weeks.

Anyone who has ever visited a racetrack knows that the kaleidoscope of racing silks becomes a blur as the horses cross the finish line. With a bit of imagination, the possibilities of transforming those same racing silks into objects for the home and fashion seem limitless— perhaps as a framed set of silks on an office wall or as a front porch flag. There are pillows, bow ties, scarves, and even mugs and mouse pads. The classic Hermès scarf was inspired by the famous French family's racing silks.

LEFT: Steeplechase jockey Danielle Hodsdon. BELOW: The silks room at Keeneland. OPPOSITE: The Jockey Club's application for silks regis-ration forms.

JACKETS

Halves	**Triangular Thirds**	**Yoke**	**(Hoop)**	**Diamond Frame**	**Old Triangular Panel**	**Old Chevrons**
		center 4 1/2 inches down from collar	4" hoop	12" X 11" frame 2" wide		8-3/4" long 1-3/8" wide 1-3/8" apart
(Solid)	**(Panel)**	**(Braces)**	**Two Hoops**	**(Diamond)**	**(Triangular Panel)**	**(Chevrons)**
plain	4" center strip (stripe)	2" vertical strip	2" wide 3" apart	10" vertical diamond	One large "V" (chevron)	Alternating 2" chevrons
Diagonal Stripes	**(Visible Seams)**	**(Cross Sashes)**	**(Multiple Hoops)**	**(Blocks)**	**(Cross of Lorraine)**	**Shamrocks**
1 1/2" alternating	1" each side of seam (seams)	4" diagonal stripe from each shoulder (cross belts)	Alternating 2 1/2" hoops (hoops)	4" squares (checks)	10" cross any style	3" scattered
(Diamonds)	**(Quartered)**	**(Epaulets)**	**(Star)**	**(Stars)**	**(Dots)**	**Hearts**
3 1/2" X 5"		2" wide 4" long	12" star	3" stars scattered	2 1/2" diameter (Spots)	3 1/2" scattered
(Stripes)	**(Ball)**	**(Vertical Halves)**	**(Sash)**	**(Diagonal Quarters)**	**(Inverted Triangle)**	**Circle**
Alternating 1 1/2" vertical stripes	10" solid ball (disc)	vertically only (halved)	4" wide left shoulder to right hip	Triangles of same size (diabolo)	10" triangle	10" circle 2" wide
(Ball Sash)	**(Diamond Hoop)**	**(Block Frame)**				
3 1/2" balls from right shoulder to left hip	3 1/2" X 5"	10" block (hollow box)				

SLEEVES

Chevrons old style 1" wide	**Two Hoops** 2" wide, 3" apart	**Circle** 5" circle 1 1/2" wide	**Diamond Seam** 3 1/2" X 5"	**Diamond Hoop** 3 1/2" X 5"	**Ball** 5" diameter	**Vertical Halves**

(Solid)	(Seams)	(Halves)	(Hoop) 4" wide	(Dots) 2 1/2"	(Chevrons) 2"	(Hoops) 2 1/2"	(Diagonal Quarters)	(Stripes) 1 1/2"	(Blocks) 4"	(Diamonds) 3 1/2" X 5"	(Stars) 3"

KEENELAND

Twice a year, in April and October, horse lovers gather at the elegant Keeneland racetrack in Lexington for an afternoon of extraordinary racing and a bowl of burgoo.

This distinctive racetrack has the ambiance of a countryside setting punctuated by a native Kentucky limestone clubhouse blanketed with Boston ivy, designed in a pattern of two small stones set over a larger stone. During the 1930s, the landscape architecture firm of Innocenti and Webel was hired to create a parklike setting. In the infield, Japanese yews in a topiary pattern gracefully spell out the word *Keeneland* in a vibrant green. Portions of the parking lots sit on the grass, and an abundance of flowering dogwood, pear, and crabapple trees throughout the area display their colors during each race meeting. Pin oaks, Yoshino cherries, sycamores, Chinese elms, and maples complete the immaculate scenery.

Led by Hal Price Headley, the Keeneland Association incorporated in 1935 and negotiated a purchase from the Keene family of 147 ½ acres off the Versailles Pike. Since then, the venue has expanded to 997 acres and now includes a Thoroughbred sales facility. Kentucky Derby winner Canonero II was a $1,200 purchase in 1971, and Fusaichi Pegasus, who sold for $4 million in 2000, also went on to win the Kentucky Derby. Designated a National Historic Landmark in 1986, Keeneland has a full calendar, with such popular races as the Blue Grass Stakes, the Lexington Stakes, the Spinster Stakes, the Queen Elizabeth II Challenge Cup, and the Royal Chase for the Sport of Kings.

The Keeneland Association is a non-dividend-paying corporation, and all profits are reinvested in the Keeneland Foundation, a charitable arm of the group, which contributes to a wide variety of worthy causes.

The Keeneland Library, founded in 1939, opened in a new 10,000-square-foot building designed by Morio Ko in 2002. With more than 10,000 volumes, 1,500 videocassettes, and 225,000 photo negatives, the library also houses the entire archival collection of the Daily Racing Form since 1896.

Finally, there's the burgoo, a thick soup steeped in history. The Turf Catering Company, which has offered the specialty since the track opened in 1936, serves up to four hundred gallons of the tasty treat each day during the racing season. Some attendees even order it to freeze and serve later.

One native says the ancient ingredients of burgoo, originally cooked in a black iron pot, consisted of "the day's take while out game-hunting"—deer, rabbit, or squirrel. Needless to say, beef is now the main ingredient.

BURGOO

Oil

3 pounds stew meat, cubed

1 teaspoon ground thyme

1 teaspoon sage

1 teaspoon oregano

1 teaspoon minced garlic

1 cup diced celery

1 cup diced carrot

1 cup diced onion

1 12-ounce can diced tomatoes in juice

2 16-ounce cans mixed vegetables

1 7-ounce can tomato puree

2 pounds fresh okra, sliced

1 tablespoon beef base

1 teaspoon Worcestershire sauce

1 cup sherry

3 pounds potatoes, diced

Cornstarch

Heat the oil in a large Dutch oven. Brown the stew meat with the herbs and garlic. Add the remaining ingredients, except the cornstarch, and cover with water. Bring to a boil, reduce the heat, and simmer for at least 3 hours. Adjust the seasonings to taste and thicken with cornstarch. Makes 10 to 12 servings.

Courtesy of Chef Ed Boutilier and Turf Catering Company

OPPOSITE, RIGHT, FROM TOP: Three paintings by Joanne Mehl.

STARBUCKS

In recent years, a well-known high-end caffeine franchise opened on Broadway, the wide retail boulevard and promenade in Saratoga Springs, New York. During the summer racing season, locals and visitors gather outside under an awning along the sidewalk to peruse the "Pink Sheet," a section of *The Saratogian* newspaper that scopes out the afternoon races. Most patrons would be surprised to know that a hundred years before the first grande caffe latte or venti dulce de leche was brewed, a Starbuck's department store was located right up the street.

Ella and Edgar Starbuck, owners of the uptown department store, moved into 11 Fifth Avenue in 1897. Two years later, they bought the lot behind the main redbrick house and built a carriage house of the same brick with access in Hall Alley, now known as Starbuck Lane. The structure included four box stalls for horses on the west side, with hay and feed storage above them. On the east side, the large open space downstairs served as carriage storage. As was true of most carriage houses of the era, the second floor was intended as groom's quarters.

The carriage house remained in the Starbuck family until 1944. It was then converted into two apartments. During the 1970s, a few cosmetic changes were made: The shed dormers on the west were changed to gable dormers, and an eyebrow dormer and a front porch were added.

In 1990, architect Tom Frost and his wife, Carole Tarantino, purchased the Starbuck carriage house and converted it to a single-family dwelling. The transformation couldn't have fallen into more capable hands; Tom specializes in restoring carriage houses, in addition to his other

architectural projects. Since receiving a master's degree in architecture from Harvard Graduate School of Design in 1966, he's renovated more than thirty carriage houses.

"I was first attracted to the building by the exterior—the brick walls, slate roof, dormers, and cupola—and, of course, the location," Tom says of his own home. "I started by converting the original carriage bay part of the house into our living room," he adds. "Before the renovation, this area was a garage with concrete floors. You could even see the grooves in the concrete that prevented the horses from slipping. Typical of carriage bays, the walls and the ceilings were finished with bead board, which I removed from the bays and walls and used only on the ceiling."

The original sliding carriage doors were fixed in place and now serve as windows into a living room filled with light and embellished with several pieces of horse-related artwork. In an upstairs loft den, Tom used sliding stall doors from another project. If a stall door or railing doesn't work well in one renovation, he can easily set it aside for another, such as his office, another former carriage house one block off Broadway in Long Alley.

"There was a high percentage of carriage houses in this town from the era of no cars, and the alleys provided access for the carriages," Tom notes. "Saratoga has a nice system of midblock alleys."

The bones of the carriage house that now accommodates Frost Architecture are immediately revealed in the rich dark spruce beaded wainscoting. A sliding stall door to the conference room shows dents and gashes from

< 148 >

years of fidgety horses kicking and biting. "The small and high window you see here and in other buildings like it tell you that's where the horses lived," Tom explains. The inaccessibility of the windows protected curious equines from potential injury.

On the second floor of Tom's office, massive exposed wooden trusses frame a work space used for drawing. This is the key architectural element in many of the two-story carriage houses Tom has adapted. In order to reduce the number of columns needed in the downstairs area and leave enough room to maneuver horses and carriages, heavy timber trusses were used to support the upper level and provide a ceiling below.

In some cases, Tom integrates existing pillars and posts into the interior plans. This was the case on North Broadway, six blocks from the modern-day Starbucks, where the character of the avenue magically becomes a grand residential pageant. A circa 1903 Gothic Revival brick residence designed by Saratoga architect R. Newton Brezee includes a wooden carriage house

Inside the carriage house, which Tom renovated, he kept a hitching post in place and salvaged iron partitions from the horses' stalls and fixed them to the central staircase.

The current owners, Blythe and Robert Clay of Three Chimneys Farm in Lexington, Kentucky, spend their mornings each August reading the latest horse news on a front porch addition that replicates the Gothic disposition of the building. "The porch columns and round

PREVIOUS PAGE: The porch addition of Robert and Blythe Clay's summer home was extended to provide a covered entrance. ABOVE, CLOCK-WISE FROM LEFT: A louvered cupola on this renovated carriage house originally provided ventilation to the hayloft. Just to the right of the cupola is a gabled dormer with dentil molding at the eaves, octagonal wood shingles, and red slate roof shingles. According to architect Tom Frost, the part of the carriage house where the horses lived can be identified by the small, high windows seen here. OPPOSITE, CLOCKWISE FROM TOP LEFT: Tom Frost. Frost's drawing for a carriage house on Woodlawn Avenue in Saratoga Springs. Frost Architecture's offices were originally a carriage house. Architect R. Newton Breeze is credited with the original design of the carriage house for 687 Broadway, which had carriage bays, box stalls, and a tack room with groom's quarters and a hayloft on the second floor. Blythe and Robert Clay read the early-morning Saratoga newspapers. The living room at 1 Starbuck Lane, once the carriage bay, was used as a garage until a 1991 renovation.

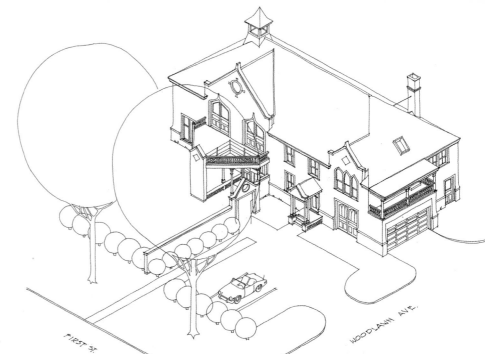

window details were copied from the main building," Tom says, "and a corner of the porch roof protects the entry while the freestanding beams and columns provide a gateway to the entry area." Once again, he preserved the carriage house doors.

Tom has also done work on the redbrick residence and carriage house on 1.39 acres at 779 North Broadway. The two-and-a-half-story mansion was built in 1881 by William Gage, a prominent Saratoga businessman and an owner of the United States Hotel; it now belongs to Texas horse owner Donald Adam. The architectural touches here intentionally embrace various design styles, from the Jacobean curved Flemish gables to oversize Elizabethan windows with heavy mullions to a Queen Anne–style patterned chimney now wrapped in ivy.

In 1986, Tom designed a decorative gazebo addition to the house, and in 2000, he adapted the companion carriage house as a guesthouse. One of the larger carriage houses in Saratoga, the original two-story building boasted a hand-operated lift that brought carriages to storage on the second floor. The lift was restored and remains in place as an architectural objet d'art.

The first floor has a kitchen, a dining room, a living room, and a billiard room. Upstairs, six bedrooms and bathrooms and a sitting room offer accommodations for the family and their guests. No detail was spared in the renovation; Tom even matched the original red slate roof from a quarry in Granville, New York. A space that once contained elegant carriages is now a three-car garage that spills onto Woodlawn Avenue.

The former half-block dirt and gravel alley, now paved, reveals a series of beguiling old structures. A Victorian clapboard storage building with multipaned side windows is now a handsome yellow garage. Farther along the street is another new carriage house.

"The carriage house is now an architectural form for new construction," Tom notes.

OPPOSITE: As part of a renovation for his carriage house/home at 1 Starbuck Lane, Tom Frost used the original sliding carriage bay doors. RIGHT, FROM TOP: Now fixed with windows, the hayloft door had a beam above (which remains in place), which was used as a pulley. The original Starbuck's in Saratoga offered dry goods, not coffee.

An August Affair

The gurgling and rejuvenating waters in the stately spa of Saratoga Springs have drawn visitors to this upstate New York venue since the eighteenth century. In 1863, Thoroughbred horse racing brought the town to life with a late-summer scene. Lillian Russell and Diamond Jim Brady frequented a number of swank gambling casinos there that operated through World War II. Since the storied track opened, each August brings pilgrims who sip from historic public fountains all around this charming community or soak at the pari-mutuel windows or in a mineral bath in its famous bathhouses.

A drink of restorative water with a whiff of sulfur might be just what the doctor ordered because a heavy dose of stamina is required to keep the pace of the social swirl. The day begins before dawn on the back side of the track as exercise riders, trainers, and owners converge in a glorious setting of rhythmic gallops. The scent of horses perfumes the usually cool morning air. Horsemen grab a bacon-and-egg sandwich at the track kitchen and the latest news from Indian Charlie's daily newsletter, along with a copy of the *Saratoga Special* newspaper.

As the sun comes up, a city worker gets out of his truck in Congress Park at the top of Union Avenue to change the begonias that spell out the date. (A new flat of flowers indicating each new date is put in place and covered with mulch.) Horticulture is a central aspect of the atmosphere. Hanging baskets of petunias embellish the ancient green barns, geraniums galore burst from window boxes on enchanting Victorian homes, and morning glories climb up lampposts.

By midmorning, authors are signing their books at the National Museum of Racing, handicappers are getting insider's tips at the *Daily Racing Form*'s seminars at the popular Siro's restaurant, and art lovers are converging at the Beresford Gallery on Union Avenue. If there's time, you can throw in a few sets of grass-court tennis at the Saratoga Golf and Polo Club or eighteen holes of golf in the state park near the Gideon Putnam Hotel.

After a sumptuous lunch at the Saratoga Reading Room, it's off to the races for most satisfied diners. In the paddock, a who's who of racing cognoscenti—Helen Kleberg Groves of the King Ranch, racehorse owner Peggy Steinman, and, of course, Marylou Whitney—gather against the backdrop of the historic red and white clubhouse to watch the horses being saddled.

Marylou has been the belle of Saratoga since 1958, when she arrived as the fourth wife of Cornelius ("Sonny") Vanderbilt Whitney. Together they stood in the winner's circle on many occasions and held court at a themed soirée for three hundred guests at the Canfield Casino. Sonny died in 1992, and five years later, Marylou married John Hendrickson. The party tradition continues.

The social calendar also includes an evening with Yo-Yo Ma or Itzhak Perlman and the Philadelphia Orchestra at the Saratoga Performing Arts Center, the National Museum of Dance and Hall of Fame Ball, the Equine Advocates Gala, and watching the action while sipping champagne over a few chukkers in the Whitney Cup at Saratoga Polo.

The annual yearling sales at the Fasig-Tipton Humphrey S. Finney Pavilion also provide a social event of sorts as hundreds of spectators gather to watch. The staccato tapping of the auction hammer startles the horse circling in a tiny roped-off area inside. President and auctioneer Walt Robertson breaks in, "There's a lot more horse here than on the board." Spotters dressed in black tie accept bids from the balcony, the telephone, and seemingly invisible bidders.

The hammer slams down.

Sold, hip number 142 . . . $2.2 million for the chestnut colt by Mr. Greeley.

Wait—it's not over yet. After the sales, there's dinner at Sperry's, the Wishing Well, Hattie's Chicken Shack, or Wheatfields, followed by partying at the Parting Glass, a late-night Irish pub. More than a few race-trackers head from the pub straight back to work in the barns after a Saratoga day and night that never seems to include a finish line.

Part IV: In the Ring

THE POSSIBILITY OF AN

Olympic gold medal looms as a distant dream for many equestrians. Only after years of disciplined training, serious subsidy, and a dash of luck do the golden rings seem within reach. When not leaping over perilously imposing multicolored obstacles, show jumper Georgina Bloomberg both epitomizes the essence of appropriate attire and ensures that others have proper riding jackets.

Correct attire is paramount for the ladies who ride sidesaddle in an event where even a glove out of place can mean the difference between a blue and a red ribbon.

In the discipline of dressage, the horse reacts to subtle cues and demonstrates time-honored leaps of faith.

A sculptor indulges her passion for horses in life-size bronze works of art, an adventurous couple creates a hunting lodge with a tropical twist, and a little girl embarks on her quest to be a star in the horse show ring. Then again, perhaps she'll follow in the footsteps of her famous father, the actor and comedian George Lopez, and display her talents in a different arena. In the meantime, Mayan Lopez and other equestrians practice daily and strengthen the unspoken bond with their horses.

OPPOSITE: Riding to win involves hours of practice and a heavy dose of patience. The results are rewarding in the form of ribbons and baubles.

<158>

2006 USEF/MARKEL
YOUNG HORSE DRESSAGE
EASTERN SELECTION TRIAL
SIX-YEAR-OLD DIVISION
CHAMPION

CLOTHESHORSE

A riding habit, no matter what the fashion happens to be, is like a uniform, in that it must be made and worn according to regulations. It must above all be meticulously trig and compact. Nothing must be sticking out a thousandth part of an inch that can be flattened in.

—Emily Post, 1922

It's an axiom in equine circles that the horse does not make the rider. The opposite is said of the rider's clothes. "In the first place, when we appear among strangers, our horsemanship, until we have an opportunity to prove it, will be appraised by those conversant in such matters by nothing less trivial than the cut of our breeches and the fit of our boots," Ivy Maddison wrote in her 1924 book, *Riding Astride for Girls.*

Georgina Bloomberg knows all about proper riding attire. As a little girl, she showed ponies at all the top horse shows, including the Devon Horse Show and Country Fair along suburban Philadelphia's Main Line. She wore jodhpurs and paddock boots while riding small ponies, and says, "Because my trainer was very strict, I had to wear my hair in pigtails [the better not to appear too tall or out of proportion with her pony for the judges] until I was about ten years old." It was about this time that Georgina got her first pair of tall boots, helping her appear more mature on larger ponies and horses.

The hunter classes in the horse shows today have evolved from an exclusive competition for foxhunters to a sport that attracts a wide variety of riders. In the 1950s, competitors in the hunter classes wore the same attire they would in the field: heavy wool jackets, canary yellow vests, and white stock ties.

"In today's hunter show ring you'll find the riders in laced field boots, primarily black, although we're seeing a comeback of the dark brown field boot," says Jill Apfel-baum, owner of Malvern Saddlery in Pennsylvania. "Breeches are varied shades of a traditional tan with a suede knee patch worn with a brown belt, and there's a wide range of acceptable colors in the traditional three-button show coat. Colors should be kept conservative and are generally in the darker range of black, navy, gray, or brown, with small plaids and pinstripes totally acceptable."

Women wear traditional ratcatcher shirts with a band collar and matching choker, frequently embroidered with an attractive monogram, worn over the neckband.

"When I rode hunters," Georgina recalls, "I always tried to choose a jacket to complement my horse's color."

For a chestnut horse, Jill recommends any dark rich brown or navy coat. "This would work with a neutral-colored shirt so as not to argue with the vivid color of this horse," she says. She strongly advises against the hot pink lining sometimes incorrectly chosen by teenage girls.

"Thinking of the total color coordination of horse and rider creates a very eye-pleasing picture for the judges as you enter the ring, where first impressions count," adds Jill, also a lifelong equestrian. According to Ivy Maddison, "While occasionally one does see a badly got-up rider put up a good performance, such an exhibition never fails to call forth surprised comment from any real horsewoman or horseman who may be present."

Proper attire in the show ring also calls for black or dark brown gloves and an approved helmet in black, dark brown, or navy blue, usually chosen to match the

<161>

coat. For the more formal jumper classes, the preferred look is white breeches with a dark coat and a white or light-colored shirt. Dress boots are more proper for the rated jumper divisions, and while gloves are not mandatory, they do complete the look.

"The clothing is important," says Ronnie Beard, a trainer and nationally recognized judge with the United States Equestrian Federation. He points out that riding attire is designed with protection and comfort in mind. "The tall boots should be a quarter-inch below the knee to protect the leg. The breeches should be a close fit, with room for bending and jumping or galloping. It should all be very conservative."

David Mielenz of Collierville Saddlery, based in Tennessee, agrees. "Show-ring attire for both men and women needs to be classic, understated, and well fitted," he says.

Georgina Bloomberg now competes on the international show jumping circuit. In just a few years she has gone from jumping ponies over 2½-foot fences to soaring effortlessly over the brightly colored red, green, and blue rails that frequently measure more than 5 feet high. Her show schedule begins each winter at her home in Wellington, Florida, where she rides and shows her jumpers, including Nadia, her brown Dutch Warmblood mare and the winner of a number of lucrative competitions at the Winter Equestrian Festival.

"When she goes in the ring, she's always all business," Bloomberg says of her twelve-year-old charge. "She's the first young horse that I brought along. I bought her when she was about five, so it's very rewarding to me, a horse like that, a horse I didn't just buy as a Grand Prix horse. She's light on her feet, and very honest."

Georgina travels throughout Europe, often riding as a member of the United States Equestrian Team. On these occasions, she wears the team's coveted red coat and a royal blue collar with white piping.

Several years ago, she started a charitable project called the Rider's Closet to help collect gently used riding clothes along with good-quality riding equipment. The items are then donated to intercollegiate riding programs around the country.

Georgina came up with the idea for the program when she started to help her father, New York City mayor Michael Bloomberg, pack up a house that had been sold. She discovered a closet full of her childhood riding clothes. "Most of the clothes were in great shape because I'd simply outgrown them," she says. "I wanted to give them to somebody, but I had no idea where to turn or what to do."

Several of her friends on the riding circuit also had closets filled with used clothing and equipment. Bevel Saddlery in New Jersey, from which Georgina orders many of her jackets, donated items as well.

"If it's something a rider has outgrown, something they don't need anymore, as long as it's in a good, usable condition, we promise we'll put it to good use," she says. "There are so many people out there that really need decent riding clothes and equipment but can't afford them. Riding is such an expensive sport. I knew we could do something about this; it was just a matter of connecting the dots. The Rider's Closet connects all of those dots."

Back in 1922, Emily Post wrote, "If you want to see a living example of perfection in riding clothes, go to the next horse show, where Miss Belle Beach is riding, and look at her!" Today, the same can be said for Georgina Bloomberg.

OPPOSITE, ABOVE LEFT: Georgina Bloomberg soars over a jump at the Washington International Horse Show. When not competing in international jumping events, Georgina works on her charity project The Rider's Closet, collecting gently used riding attire for aspiring equestrians. OPPOSITE, BELOW LEFT: Artist Henry Kohler's *Boot Maker's Shop Corner.*

James and Mary Lea Treptow
on behalf of
The Fauquier Hospital Foundation

cordially invites you to the

"Wall of Honor" Luncheon
at the
Upperville Colt and Horse Show

Saturday,
June 9, 2007
11:30am - 2:30pm

Upperville Horse Show Grounds
at the Tent next to the Grand Stands
Route 50
Upperville, Virginia

This is not a fundraiser;
no contributions are being requested.

UCHS
FRIEND

The Detroit Horse Show
THE BLOOMFIELD OPEN HUNT
BLOOMFIELD HILLS, MICHIGAN 48013

CLASS 49

50th ANNIVERSARY
B.O.H.

HAMPTON CLASSIC
1999
Crown Royal
THE LEGENDARY IMPORT
rider/trainer
ADMIT ONE

PAS DE DEUX

The equestrian discipline of dressage dates to the Greeks and Romans, when horses used in battle displayed the suppleness and flexibility to turn, the discipline to obey commands, and, most important, a strong sense of bravery. As horses leaped into the air on cue, in a movement known as the *capriole,* warriors were able to elude enemy weapons and inflict damage of their own.

Susie Dutta can attest to the intricacies of dressage. A world-class dressage competitor living in Wellington, Florida, she spends five to six hours each day perfecting the timeless dance in movements called piaffe, passage, and half-pass. She has five horses in training with an eye on the Olympics and a young son, Timmy, whose schedule is full with school, tae kwon do classes, golf lessons, and playdates.

When Susie and her husband, Tim, bought their Florida home, she called on designer Susan Rubin, who has a shop called Beyond the Barn, to help her decorate. "We met in the winter season of 1999," Susan recalls. "She was a customer who had just purchased a home in Binks Forest and wanted to decorate everything horsey. We started talking in May of 2000 at the Raleigh Horse Show and immediately made plans to order her dining set and to start the transformation from a plain vanilla home to equine chic."

They studied the floor plan. The formal living room became the dining room, with room to seat twelve comfortably. "We started with paint and colors," Susan says. The walls are finished with Ralph Lauren Cheyenne Rock paint in a suede texture. A chandelier in a foxhunting motif is the room's focal point. The dining table and hutch were custom made and have a rubbed wax finish. The chairs, six with arms and four without, were painted in a full range of Crayola colors chosen for a "playful look." Each chair has a custom-sewn foxhunt tapestry chair pad with tassels. If a guest comes in with mud on his or her derrière after a day of riding horses, it's not the end of the world because the pads are easily cleaned.

A large apple-green armoire was chosen to finish the room and store linens, glassware, and serving dishes. Pictured in a painting by artist Judy Weider on the far wall in the dining room is Susie's first Grand Prix horse, Maple Magnum.

The home's original dining room became an office for Tim, who has a horse transport business. "I chose Ralph Lauren Dressage wallpaper in navy blue to accent the back wall," Susan says. "We framed major win photos and added brass bars to decorate the office wall."

They ordered furniture from the local Office Depot. A leather loveseat from the Duttas' collection provided ample seating. A Ralph Lauren fabric that matches the wallpaper was sewn into pleated panels to finish the office window.

Just steps away, a large kitchen opens to a family area. This is where the Duttas begin their day. "I get up and have coffee with my son and all of our animals," Susie says. "I turn on the fish-tank light and feed the fish. Change the lights around on the lizard. Feed him. Then the dogs, Daisy and Teacup, rule the backyard for the morning. I love the mornings, and we get up a little earlier so we can enjoy them. My son loves to watch the birds, and we identify most of them with his bird book."

<164>

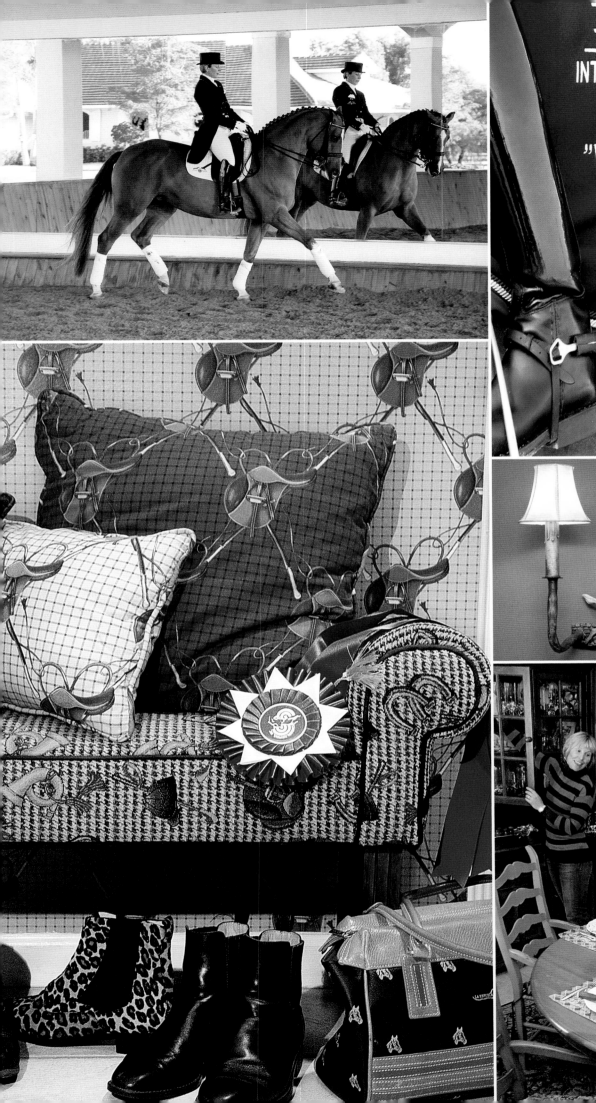

'N EVERGLADES

Guests at Phyllis and Paul Rosen's Mediterranean revival home in South Florida enter a courtyard and pass a life-size cast-stone alligator leering from beneath an Italian terra-cotta bench. Potted gardenia trees flank the French front doors, and vivid fuchsia and coral bougainvillea reach out over the custom color Rose Clay walls.

Their home, 'N Everglades, is a tropical hunting lodge filled with fascinating collections of horse-related china, art, and furnishings. "It doesn't garner images of the rolling fields in Virginia," says Phyllis, a lifelong horse lover and artist. She has used their house as a blank canvas to transfer the sporting life of English foxhunts to the Sunshine State.

The Rosens grew up within blocks of each other in the Miami suburbs of Dade County, but never met as youngsters. They both enjoyed outdoor sports; Paul played tennis in high school and college, and Phyllis was busy riding horses.

Paul was a business major at the University of Miami and later took over his family's commercial property investments. Phyllis studied art and theater at the University of Miami at the same time, but their paths still never crossed in Coral Gables.

Introduced by a cousin, Phyllis and Paul finally met in the spring of 1971 and married six weeks later. They honeymooned by taking in the Wimbledon Tennis Championships outside London and the Aachen Horse Show in Germany.

While newlyweds, the Rosens settled near Key Biscayne "so Paul could have a boat," Phyllis recalls. She continued to ride and eventually persuaded him to tag along to the horse shows. Not much of a spectator, Paul became smitten with horses himself and decided to learn to ride.

The Rosens eventually bought a horse farm in Aiken, South Carolina, where both rode with the Whiskey Road Foxhounds and the Aiken Hounds and had several national champion show hunters. When not at the barn with their horses or at a horse show, the Rosens began to scour flea markets, antique shows, and shops for horse-related items.

"We purchased our first plate for fifteen dollars in Ybor City during the Tampa Horse Show," Phyllis says. "When we were newlyweds in Miami, nobody wanted antiques. They were knocking down houses on Miami Beach in those days. We bought a bronze and copper chandelier from a grand old house that has been in three houses with us now."

Now the Rosens have returned to their roots in South Florida. In the past thirty years, they've brought back items from England and other European countries and from the famous flea market in Brimfield, Massachusetts. Their collection includes dozens of china patterns, Dutch painted soda glass, and Victorian jasperware. They own three hundred pieces of Royal Bayreuth Hunting and Coaching Scenes, highly prized by equestrian folks, keeping this cherished collection in a custom-built lighted display case.

Royal Bayreuth china was originally manufactured in Bavaria and dates from 1880 to 1920. The scenes include foxhunting, sidesaddle, fly fishing, and other country pursuits. The Rosens have gathered vases, urns, pitchers, miniature creamers, and match holders, all finished in strong shades of yellow and green.

<167>

The Rosens eat breakfast in their expansive open kitchen as their beagles, Chevy and Bertie (named after characters on the BBC *Lovejoy* series about an unscrupulous antique dealer), look on. The walls have been washed in five shades of pink, salmon, and ochre. Phyllis painted the finials on the ends of the curtain rods in a capricious pattern of tropical leaves, and a plate rail above the windows holds a series of eighteen English stoneware foxhunting plates made by Cauldon in the late 1800s. The edges of each plate are painted in an ochre color.

Paul regularly thumbs through catalogs from auction houses, where he may find a particular piece of art he wants to pursue. The bronze horse sculpture on the center island, by Antoine-Louis Barye (1796–1875), was a gift from Phyllis's parents, also longtime devoted collectors of fine art. "I call it *Spent*," says Phyllis, "because he looks exhausted."

Barye was among a group of French sculptors known as Les Animaliers. A onetime goldsmith and engraver, he brought movement to his work at a time when most artists had idealized rigid studies of man and beast. Barye attended classes at l'École des Beaux-Arts and frequently

ABOVE: Phyllis Rosen's whimsical sketch portrays a human handbag on the female alligator's arm. CLOCKWISE FROM TOP RIGHT: Hunting whips and horse-show photos are displayed on an equestrian-themed wrought-iron console table. Phyllis painted the finials on the ends of the curtain rods. The plate rail above holds English stoneware foxhunting plates made by Cauldon in the late 1800s. A slip-decorated Jasperware cheese dome, circa 1880. The bronze sculpture on the center island of the kitchen (at left) was a gift from Phyllis's parents. The Rosens' collection of English pottery includes a water pitcher filled with Florida firecracker.

visited the zoo in Paris, where keepers often gave him carcasses so he could scrutinize animal anatomy.

Barye's clients included dignitaries of society and royalty. He went on to become a curator at the Louvre, where several pieces of his work can now be found.

Romanian sculptor Constantin Cristesco created another bronze owned by the Rosens, *Cheval sautant l'obstacle* ("Horse Jumping a Fence"), between 1900 and 1930. A riderless horse is jumping over a post-and-rail obstacle in graceful form. A small marble mounting as a backdrop complements the deep brown patina.

For a luncheon party at 'N Everglades, guests might be served on the bone china made by Wedgwood in England for Phillips Ltd. at 43 and 44 New Bond Street. The Jorrocks series has a gilt rim and a beaded edge called "lamb's tongue." The whimsical plates include such drily humorous titles as "A Showy, Washy, Useless Beast."

Artist John Leech created the illustrations on the plates as well as etchings and woodcut political cartoons for a number of British magazines, including *Punch* and *Illustrated London News.* He brought the humorous master of foxhounds Jorrocks, created by writer Robert Smith Surtees (1803–1864), to life with his caricatures. Surtees wrote a series of stories about Jorrocks for the *New Sporting Magazine* that were later collected in a popular book, *Jorrocks's Jaunts and Jollities,* published in London in 1869. While the vintage editions are quite precious, a paperback version was published in 2006.

Another of the Rosens' equestrian-inspired china acquisitions is a black-and-white hunting-scene luncheon set manufactured by Copeland Spode in England in the 1880s. The wide rim is finished in flat beaded style, and the pattern on each plate is different; examples include "Throwing Off" and "The Kill." When setting the table, Phyllis pairs them with small black-and-white checked place mats.

The Rosens' china collection is so vast that they display some of it on the top shelves in Paul's walk-in closet. His intense interest in the subject of sporting art, especially the work of British artist Sir Alfred Munnings (1878–1959), is manifest here. Leather-bound editions of Munnings's autobiographical trilogy—*An Artist's Life, The Second Burst,* and *The Finish*—are treasured tomes.

A Munnings painting, *Horses in a Stream,* hangs in the den. The artist's work is coveted by serious collectors of this genre. One of the highest prices ever paid for a Munnings painting was $7,848,000. Known as *The Red Prince Mare,* it was sold by Sotheby's in New York in May 2004 from the collection of Mr. and Mrs. John Hay Whitney.

Munnings liked to paint *en plein air,* frequently taking his canvases on excursions in the English countryside. Bringing along his ponies and a groom, he strove to capture the ever-changing light in the meadows and streams.

The books by Munnings in the large closet are but a hint of the furnishings of Paul's sporting life. A yoga mat (used daily) is rolled up near a formal hunting jacket and vest draped over a cane seat chair. The needlepoint hunting belt and the sherbet-colored short-sleeve cotton polo shirts from Robert Redd are Florida staples.

Cowboy boots, popular plaid Burberry rain boots, and canvas-topped Newmarket boots await informal occasions. The familiar military green Wellington boots hail from the Hunter Boot Company, which holds the coveted Royal Warrant. They were originally designed in leather to the specifications of the Duke of Wellington in 1817. Farmers from Florida to Maine as well as British aristocrats now wear them.

The lady of the house has her own collection of footwear out by the back door. A circa 1880 mahogany Victorian hall tree spills over with a collection of canes with horn, bamboo, and scrimshaw handles. There are horse-show ribbons, hats galore, and, of course, boots. Phyllis uses them not only for riding but also for walking through the flea markets and antique shops around the world.

"We go on stuff-hunting trips," Phyllis says.

PREVIOUS PAGES: The Rosens' many pieces of equestrian-inspired china. LEFT, FROM TOP: Pieces from an assemblage of Royal Bayreuth "Hunting and Coaching Scenes" spill over to the top shelves in Paul Rosen's closet. The furnishings of a gentleman's sporting life include a formal hunting jacket, cowboy boots, Burberry boots, and canvas-topped Newmarket boots. A needlepoint belt with horses is a must for any sporting gentleman. OPPOSITE: Phyllis has her own collection of footwear, hats, and canes on a Victorian mahogany hall tree.

LADIES' NIGHT

The history of ladies riding sidesaddle goes back as far as the ninth century. (In certain social circles, particularly among the landed gentry and aristocracy, it was considered in poor taste for a woman to ride astride— that is, with one leg on each side of the horse.) The saddle is oriented to the left side, going back to the days when a woman sat sideways in her long dress behind a man. In 1382, England's Anne of Bohemia, wife of Richard II, used one of the first versions of the actual sidesaddle, a heavily padded object at the time.

Some equestriennes would testify that riding and jumping a horse while *astride* is difficult enough. For Jeanne Blackwell, Sandra Forbush, and Lisa Friel, the art of riding *aside* has an allure that combines athletic accomplishment with the romance of a bygone era.

When Jeanne Blackwell was a horse-crazy little girl in the mid-1960s, she attended the Washington International Horse Show at the D.C. Armory. The October event is one of the final indoor international jumping events of the season.

Jeanne found herself mesmerized during a break in the evening performance. While visiting the powder room, she watched a chic woman getting ready for the Ladies' Side Saddle class apply bright red lipstick and fold her hair neatly under a hairnet. The woman had on a yellow vest and a white stock tie, a black jacket, dark breeches, tall black boots, and a heavy black wool apron wrapped around her waist in a complicated manner. She put on a silk top hat and pulled a veil down across her face.

The little girl ran to the edge of the ring to watch. "Right then and there, I knew I had to learn how to ride sidesaddle," Jeanne recalls forty years later.

Since that first peek at the big time, Jeanne has devoted her life to horses at her 65-acre Madcap Farm in The Plains, Virginia, where she gives riding lessons and operates a boarding and training facility to support her horse habit. Each day begins the same, feeding horses and mucking out stalls. Jeanne also judges small horse shows. Her love of vintage riding attire led her to open Trouvails Vintage Collection, selling vintage handbags, evening gowns, and other treasures at trunk shows and by appointment.

In early 2004, Jeanne began her quest to master the intricacies of riding sidesaddle. She is entirely self-taught. "I went and bought the stuff and started doing it by trial and error, picking up pointers along the way."

Jeanne's determination to follow her dream of competing in sidesaddle classes at the Washington Horse Show, now held at the Verizon Center in the middle of the city, finally came to fruition in the fall of 2006. This time it was her turn to get dressed for the event. "It takes me three hours with my makeup and clothes," she says of the preparatory ritual. Before she enters the ring, the horse also has been brushed by a groom, who braids the mane and tail and tacks up the mare.

Artist Sandra Forbush watched with interest as Jeanne performed at the show. She took notes and made sketches as the judges made sure the riders were wearing the proper attire.

<175>

The ladies' riding habit and tack are known as "appointments." Traditions and horse-show rules dictate that everything must be ever so proper: A pair of white string gloves is placed under the girth on the left side with just the tips of the gloves showing. These nonslippery gloves are used instead of the proper brown leather gloves in case of rain. Each lady has a brown leather sandwich case, which must contain a small, simple sandwich (butter only, hold the mayo) on crustless white bread. It must be wrapped in a cloth handkerchief or in wax paper.

Sandra knows all about proper attire when it comes to riding sidesaddle, a discipline that also was her passion until she broke her back in a car accident. "That put a quick stop to riding," she says. "I just couldn't physically handle or manage that workload."

People started to ask Sandra to paint their dogs in pastel. "I bought a set of oils that I kept for a year before using them because I was so intimidated by them," she says. Once Sandra got going with the oils, she had countless commissions to paint horses, dogs, and people.

Sandra and her husband, Gus Forbush, a horseman and owner of a steel and crane company, share a white frame house nestled into 75 rolling acres at Foxhall Farm near Flint Hill, Virginia.

Despite her painting, Sandra's heart remains with the sidesaddle ladies. She is an expert on the proper appointments. "As for a sidesaddle portrait, it isn't different in any aspect other than you have to know the proper attire," Sandra says. "What's considered improper? An example is letting your right toe peek out from under your apron. The apron should be in a straight vertical line to the ground, with only your left heel and boot showing. The appointments are very important to have right in a painting."

Sandra begins her portraits by taking photographs with her digital Nikon camera. "Sometimes when you photograph people for paintings, you have to correct some of these little things to make them proper," she notes. "I take many pictures of my subject and sometimes have to make a painting with several pictures. If it's a horse, I use the head from one picture and the body from another."

Just as Sandra might compose a painting using many photographs, sidesaddle competitor Lisa Friel of Alexandria, Virginia, has gathered her vintage habit and appointments from several sources. "I bought my favorite sidesaddle habit on eBay," she relates. "It's a black tailcoat and matching apron made in 1917 by one of my favorite habit makers, Nardi. I actually own about nine sidesaddle habits and a few extra jackets. There are new sidesaddle habits you can buy now, but I wouldn't wear one even if it was free. They're not as nicely made in terms of the style and fabric."

According to Lisa, a new sidesaddle riding habit can cost up to $6,000; a vintage one typically costs about $500. "A friend pulled a jacket out of a Dumpster and gave it to me," she says. "I took it home and found the matching apron in my closet. I'd purchased it for thirty-two dollars on eBay years ago and never worn it. Custom-made clothes of all types often have a tag that lists the owner's name, item number, and date made. That's how you can tell if the pieces match and other information about their provenance." Both of her finds had the same maker's tag—Williams & Cleaver—and were made as matching pieces for the same lady.

Her luck on eBay continued when she bought a rare piggyback sandwich case for $900. "That included the postage to ship it from London," she says. "I've seen the same sandwich case in secondhand tack shops for nineteen hundred dollars and on up to about twenty-six hundred. It's one of my greatest treasures."

PREVIOUS PAGES: Sidesaddle rider Jeanne Blackwell. The ladies line up for sidesaddle class at the Upperville Colt and Horse Show. OPPOSITE, CLOCKWISE FROM TOP RIGHT: Sandra Forbush's oil painting of sidesaddle rider Dawn Colgan. All the sidesaddle appointments down to the crustless sandwich must be perfectly in place. Gus Forbush installed skylights in his wife's art studio when she took up painting full-time. Vintage tack and accessories such as this sandwich case can still be found on eBay. Jeanne Blackwell and Miss Brittney won several ribbons in the sidesaddle competition at the Washington International Horse Show.

HAVEN FOR LITTLE GIRLS

Mayan Lopez began her equestrian career on the back of a real live pony at Griffith Park in Los Angeles. Her mother, Ann Lopez, a casting director, and her father, comedian George Lopez, could have taken her on the circa 1926 merry-go-round, with its sixty-eight wooden horses and their fancy jeweled bridles. After all, Daddy is allergic to horses. The carousel even has a Stinson 165 military band organ, touted as "the largest band organ accompanying a carousel on the West Coast," with fifteen hundred selections of marches and waltz music.

Five-year-old Mayan had an interest in music, but not in conjunction with a wooden horse. She gravitated to the real ponies and was smitten immediately. From atop the fuzzy pony, she waved and laughed.

Now, with her child approaching her teenage years, Ann Lopez and her friend Nancy Nickerson are horse-show mothers in the sport of stand-around-and-wait while their daughters Mayan and Gabby compete, often at the Los Angeles Equestrian Center near Griffith Park. They're there to wipe off their kids' dusty boots, offer them a sip of water (only) when requested, and provide a steady stream of unlimited encouragement.

Mayan's big chestnut, Galileo, is better known as Leo around the stable. Galileo has helped furnish the ever-expanding collection of prize ribbons scattered around Mayan's playroom.

It could be called Mayan's Magical Playroom—and it's all horse. On a worktable in the far corner, a book report on *Black Beauty,* by Anna Sewell, includes photos and sketches pasted on green posterboard. Her father stayed up to help his daughter complete it on time, making the cardboard cart pulled by a tiny black horse.

Storage space for all the model horses has been streamlined with pull-out baskets that fit into cubbyholes. It's an international assortment. The small horses known as the Pony Club are made by a company in Great Britain called ELC. The jumpers are made in Germany by Schleich. The regal horses ridden by the knights hail from Papo, a French company. (For horse-crazy little girls, the origin of the toys is as important as the manufacturer of sneakers is for boys of all ages.) A collection of American Girl horses—including the palomino and Jackson the Horse—stand on top. Posters and photographs of—what else?—horses adorn the walls.

A pine armoire holds paper for homework and crafts projects, and a bookshelf contains an assortment of Breyer horses and books with titles such as *Riding, Horses and Ponies,* and *The Trail of Painted Ponies.*

Ample floor space gives Mayan room to set up a miniature barn with a corral full of horses. All the necessary miniature tools—wheelbarrow, shovel, and pitchfork—offer opportunities to "play horse."

"She can have three or four friends over, and they play for hours. It's their haven," says Ann. The animal-print club chairs can be pushed aside so Mayan can exercise her other passions: acting and singing.

It has been a busy week for Mayan. She performed on her horse in the ring and appeared on the stage in the

RIGHT: Collecting equestrian memorabilia begins at a very young age. Mayan Lopez's riding career began on top of a pony at Griffith Park in Los Angeles. BELOW: In the playroom, Mayan is able to indulge her fascination with horses and later clear the floor in order to practice for the school musical. OPPOSITE: During a horse show at the Los Angeles Equestrian Center, Mayan and her big chestnut, Galileo, await the results.

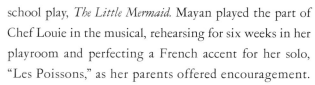

school play, *The Little Mermaid.* Mayan played the part of Chef Louie in the musical, rehearsing for six weeks in her playroom and perfecting a French accent for her solo, "Les Poissons," as her parents offered encouragement.

As the week comes to a close, Ann and George host a few friends and neighbors for dinner: Susan Duff, whose daughter Hilary is well known to all teenagers; producer Elizabeth Fowler, who grew up with Ann in Fort Lauderdale; Ann's good friend Nancy; and Ann's mother, Norda Serrano.

George spent the afternoon playing golf with buddies Andy Garcia and Roy Disney III. Actor Ken Howard and musician Dave Stewart join the group for a Lopez family favorite, arroz con pollo.

After dinner, everyone gathers around as Mayan presents an encore of her solo: "*Les poissons, les poissons,* how I love *les poissons* . . . ," she sings with a lilting French inflection. There is applause all around.

And if Mayan had to choose between a career with horses or show business, what would she do? "I'd find a part where I have to ride a horse," she says, and beams.

High-Stepping Friends

Mayan Lopez and many girls coast to coast collect model horses. For girls who cannot own or ride their own horse, the models remind them of the real thing, with no need to muck out stalls. Breyer model horses, in production since 1950, have become iconic.

The Breyer Company never planned to craft model horses. Now known as Breyer Animal Creations, a division of Reeves International, the company started on the path to worldwide success with a modest order to produce a mold for a plastic Western-style horse to be mounted on mantel clocks for the old F. W. Woolworth five-and-dime general stores.

The statuettes produced were an exact likeness, and Breyer was launched into the equine toy market with their hand-painted artisan creations. In the past sixty years, Breyer has become a household name, representing almost every equestrian hero, from the legendary Black Beauty to 2006 Kentucky Derby winner Barbaro.

Each model is intricately tailored to the physique and attitude of its equine counterpart. Artisans commit countless hours of labor and energy to molding an accurate form that matches colors, marking patterns, movements, and disposition.

The original 1950s models, known as *decorator models,* were done in exotic colors like Wedgwood blue; others had glossy finishes. Today Breyer produces several series of models; the traditional horses, crafted from plastic resin, vary in scale from one-eighth to one-ninth actual horse size. A more upscale "connoisseur" series offers intricately crafted images in limited editions.

Retail prices range from $40 to $60, yet some of these highly prized collectible models sell on auction websites for $800 to $1,500.

Kathleen Moody, an equestrian and artist based in Arizona, has probably created more Breyer models than any other living sculptor. Artisan Susan Carlton Sifton of California is famous for her lifelike racing models of champion Thoroughbreds Cigar, Ruffian, and Smarty Jones.

Three hundred new horses are created each year. The artists begin with a storyboard. They consider various themes: racing, jumping, Western, or English. The illustrator presents sketches, followed by a model in clay. The model then goes to a mold master, who creates the resin mold used in mass production.

Every Breyer horse retains a small hole from casting, typically located in the nostril, because the models have to "breathe." Without the hole, the models would bloat like balloons due to the resin material, which expands from excessive heat unless allowed to ventilate.

In the final stages, the model is assessed for stability. Twenty individual artisans are involved by the time the model goes to a decorator for completion. Each year, more than five million horses are sold. The normal production schedule for a Breyer horse is between eighteen and twenty-four months.

Part V: On the Move

THE SPORTING LIFE WITH HORSES

embraces traditions and rituals. The day begins at dawn and doesn't end until . . . Horse owners are constantly on the move, yet they refuse to budge from well-worn schedules and habits. Some horsemen still decline to use the modern conveniences of a wheelbarrow or a hose, preferring a basket and a bucket. Others have embraced every innovation from equine acupuncture to aquatic aerobic exercise for their beloved charges, showing that pampering their horses is as important as pampering themselves.

In the time one can say "coast to coast," a champion racehorse commutes on a red-eye from California's Santa Anita racetrack to Churchill Downs in Kentucky. Equestrian style emerges up close and personal for one trainer and a pretty gray pony in a unique space in a barn converted to the trainer's living quarters. Not far away, an entertainment entrepreneur brings her love of horses to Hollywood, and in Florida, a passionate collector can choose from her collection of 150 carriages when she takes her horses out for a Sunday drive.

OPPOSITE, CLOCKWISE FROM TOP LEFT: Blacksmith Joe Sitton crafts custom-designed farm signs. California architect Hap Gilman is credited for the design of a rustic barn where the horses live very close to their trainer. Wearing the proper hat is important while driving a coach. Royal Doulton coaching plates are highly collectible. Racehorses must be cooled down with a walk after early morning workouts. Horses have always been a part of life in Beverly Hills. CENTER: The buttons on the back of the livery indicate rank.

THE HORSE IN SNOWDEN'S ROOM

Harry had a horse in his room. Nobody knew. He could ride him in a circle without knocking over the chair or the dresser. He could jump him over the bed without hitting his head on the ceiling.

—Syd Hoff, *The Horse in Harry's Room* (1970)

It has always been fashionable to blur the boundaries between indoor and outdoor space in the transition from house to garden.

But home to barn?

Well, that's a house of a different color. Just ask horseman Snowden Clarke, who lives in a converted barn in California's ever-so-exclusive Sullivan Canyon equestrian neighborhood off Sunset Boulevard between Brentwood and Pacific Palisades. The residences along the private Old Ranch Road have barns and stables, most of them small, with one or two horses.

The Sullivan Canyon Preservation Association encompasses its own riding rings, jumps, and trails, all on the 8 acres given to the association by director and producer Steven Spielberg and actress Kate Capshaw when they purchased the land in 2002 for $12 million. Capshaw, her children, and other members of the association have the privilege of riding here each afternoon. Neighbors descend the steep road for a lesson or short hack-around.

A third-generation horseman originally from Virginia, Snowden now rides and teaches in this area. He learned to canter and jump on a feisty pony his grandfather imported from England. "All he did was bite and kick," Snowden recalls.

Snowden's biography reads like a horseman's Hollywood script. He once taught a Saudi prince to ride in

three days, he gave lessons to Jacqueline Kennedy Onassis, and his wide circle of friends includes the local blacksmith, the socialites and diplomats of Washington, D.C., and the powers-that-be in LA. He feels equally at ease having breakfast at a truck stop and lunch at the Polo Lounge of the Beverly Hills Hotel.

He rides and trains horses for the show ring and the hunt field as well as coaches riders of all ages. Most of his horse career unfolded in the abundant horse country of Virginia, save for nine years living in England, which included a stint at the Royal Mews in Ascot. One day, he took Horace Greeley's advice and decided to abandon the rolling Virginia hills and head west, young man.

Just like that, he cleared out his barn, packed up a trailer of horses and ponies, and found a temporary tenant for his Virginia home (in case he might return one day). Even though his Virginia farmhouse was small, California presented its own housing challenge. Sullivan Canyon is one of the most expensive areas in the country, so he decided to move into the barn with his horses.

A sloping roof stretches over one side of the barn. The walls are built from old railroad ties that are exposed on the interior. Once a tack room, the main living space was in need of a makeover. One of Snowden's first phone calls on arriving in California was to British actress-turned-designer Kathryn Ireland, whose clients include boldface

names such as Victoria Tennant and Steve Martin. Kathryn's "ease of living" style helped blur the lines between horse and human home. And she was familiar with cozy equestrian style after decorating her own 50-acre farm in France.

The front door of the "house" stands halfway down the barn aisle. Living, sleeping, and eating areas flow seamlessly in the open plan of the house. Though technically an interior space, the house has no shortage of natural materials. The floors are made of large pavers of gray slate and extend to the back patio through a large glass sliding door that reinforces the sense of cohesiveness. An outdoor picnic table, steps away from a paddock, is a perfect alfresco setting for lunch, dinner, or drinks. The horses live in a nearby barn just around the corner. Snowden is quick to speak to any nearby horse who doesn't mind his manners.

The wooden railroad ties also comprise interior walls and structural beams in the ceiling. Windows and sliding glass doors take up more than half of the wall space, providing views of the surrounding trees and bushes. Some wall space was preserved for artwork and photos. "Snowden's personal photographs were the most important objects to include," Kathryn says.

Painted with a whimsical foxhunter illustration by Snowden's friend and new neighbor Baby deSelliers, the industrial-style white venetian blinds shade three windows on the back wall. Track lighting over the bed and in the sitting area and the kitchen separately illuminates the spaces, defining them without physical barriers. The large fireplace in the corner is constructed with small stones and blends into the slate floors.

Most of the furniture came from Snowden's home in Virginia, including a large bed. "This was the biggest splurge," Kathryn says. She outfitted it with bedding

CLOCKWISE FROM TOP LEFT: Snowden Clarke's Rock Ridge Farm colors have been monogrammed onto the saddlecloths. The right side of the rustic barn designed by Hap Gilman has an apartment. Snowden and friends take a lunch break. When Snowden moved his horse business to California he brought along his farm sign from Virginia. The area of Sullivan Canyon was developed and designed by noted architect Cliff May.

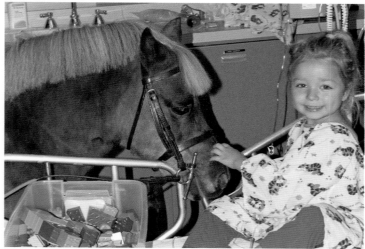

made from John Robshaw Textiles called Mandu-Lapis and Madura-Lapis. The block prints, batik, and bold patterns evoke the colors and culture of India, Thailand, and Indonesia. To coordinate with all of the natural materials and colors, Kathryn chose a scheme that included light blue bedding with a brown medallion pattern.

She used numerous pillows to create a daybed for extra seating, along with leather folding chairs from Argentina. Storage in such a small space is always an issue, so vintage trunks paired with modern pieces from IKEA offer storage solutions and tabletop space.

Kathryn suggested that Snowden hang pots and pans on the wall and use the open shelving for plates and glasses.

"It's a working barn that happens to be where I live," Snowden says.

CONCOURS D'ÉLÉGANCE

The English Stage

And high bred teams

Will soon exist

But in our dreams

—Elizabeth Cook, 1869

Gloria Austin is surrounded by horses—live and on canvas—in her offices at the Florida Carriage Museum and Resort in Central Florida. The 395-acre complex includes cottages and spacious suites for equestrians and barns and spacious stalls for equines. There are tennis courts and putting greens for horse owners and wooded driving paths and shaded paddocks for horses. A carriage museum, an education center, and the nonprofit Equine Heritage Institute, whose mission is to "promote and preserve the history of the horse and wheeled transportation," complete the facility.

As a retired executive of the New York City franchise of Paychex, a payroll service founded by her former husband, Gloria runs her horse business in a similarly efficient manner.

Why did she take up driving horses?

"A-g-e," she replies, leaning forward. "The rigors of riding are more demanding. With driving, there's no bouncing up and down."

Gloria grew up on a 1,000-acre farm in upstate New York and was entranced by the television horses of her youth—the mounts ridden by Roy Rogers, the Cisco Kid, and the Lone Ranger. Her father was a cattle dealer, and she learned to ride on a draft horse.

"I begged my father for a saddle horse," she says. "That's all I wanted."

After raising a family and establishing her career, Gloria returned to horses. In 1984, she retired to Florida and started to collect carriages and learn to drive. "Now I can sit on top of the carriage and enjoy my horses and the view," she says of the horse sport that includes coaching, combined driving, international competition, and pleasure driving. She has won numerous awards, including the North American Four-in-Hand and Coaching Championship, and she was one of the first women to drive a coach-and-four at the prestigious Newport, Rhode Island, coaching event.

A tour through her museum (open to the public six days a week) reveals a dazzling display of more than 150 horse-drawn vehicles from the United States and Europe: coaches, breaks, gigs, phaetons, runabouts, road carts, and sleighs. The commercial vehicles include a milk wagon and a peddler's wagon.

The museum's prize pièce de résistance is the 1850 Armbruster Golden Carriage Dress Chariot of Emperor Franz Josef I and Empress Elizabeth I of Austria. The Imperial Mews of the Hapsburgs in Vienna stabled hundreds of horses and carriages at Schönbrunn Palace. Hundreds of footmen, coachmen, and grooms also worked there full-time, and when the empire collapsed, some of the carriages were sold. Many of the remaining carriages from the Hapsburg collection can now be seen at the Hapsburg Museum near Vienna.

When Gloria purchased the imperial carriage from a dealer in Oregon, it was in terrible disrepair. Little is known of the 150-year provenance of the vehicle other than the fact that after making its way to the United States, it was used in the 1937 film *The Prisoner of Zenda.*

Gloria turned to Patrick Schroven of Belgium, an expert in carriage restoration, to return the chariot to its former glory. He spent a year doing research before beginning the work, using historical records and old drawings and photographs for an accurate rendition of the carriage.

The entire carriage was rebuilt, and the silk upholstery was reproduced to closely match the original. Everything down to the piping and tassels is authentic, including the lace re-created by the Rudy Stief shop in Neusass, Germany.

"It was woven on a Jacquard épinglé loom, which uses punched cards to convey the pattern," the restorer reports. "The lace is woven at seven inches per hour, and thirty-two meters were required. It was woven with the pattern of the crown of Rudolf the Second alternating with the Austrian coat of arms running horizontal and vertical."

The cushions were refilled with horsehair and sea grass. The wool carpets on the interior are matched with original patterns. There are ivory fittings and a special place

LEFT, FROM TOP: The term "four-in-hand" refers to the four reins held while driving four horses. The groom's buttons on the back of their livery denote rank. The head groom wears four; other grooms wear six. All passengers wear an apron over their lap to keep the dust from the road off their garments. OPPOSITE: Gloria Austin's Roof Seat Break is a sporting vehicle used for picnicking and driving in the park.

'*Driving* is an all-encompassing word for the discipline of driving horses, either singly or in multiples, put to any type of vehicle,' says Charles Matheson, a past president of The Coaching Club of America, founded in 1874. '*Coaching* refers to a specific discipline of handling a four-in-hand or team of horses driven to either a road coach or a park drag.'

for one's calling card. Twelve coats of paint and lacquer were used in the renovation, which took thirty months.

Gloria points out a rare Chinese cart, which she purchased on eBay and had shipped from Iowa in the back of a pickup truck. Historians have dated it as early as 1780. Coaches always were driven by staff, but a group of four-wheeled phaetons, used for sport and pleasure, were initially driven by the owner.

While Gloria dresses for a drive, it takes four grooms several hours to prepare the horses. The harness must be spotless, and the horses are cleaned and their manes braided. The buttons on the back of the grooms' livery denote rank: The head groom wears four; other grooms wear six. "The fewer buttons they have to sit on, the higher their rank," Gloria explains.

The attire worn by all members on the vehicle is just as important as the harness on the horses. Tradition dictates that ladies must wear brown leather gloves. In case of rain, white cotton string gloves, which prevent the reins from slipping, are placed just under the seat with the fingertips showing. All drivers and passengers wear an apron over their lap to keep the dust from the road off their garments. Gloria's wool lap robe is monogrammed with the letter *A*.

According to tradition, hats must be proper for both season and time of day. Straw is appropriate in spring and summer. Fur is acceptable in the winter. A brimless cocktail hat is worn at night, and rain gear is stowed inside the carriage. In competitions throughout the world, an award known as *concours d'élégance* emphasizes and rewards correct yet refined turnout. Gloria has been honored with the award on many occasions.

Katie Whaley has made many of Gloria's hats. A North Carolina custom milliner for more than twenty years, she also is a driving enthusiast. She found her niche when her own hats were admired and then coveted by fellow competitors. Her creations now appear in the closets of Oprah Winfrey, Joan Lunden, Martha Stewart, and Stefanie Powers.

Gloria reminisces about growing up on her family's farm: "My parents never asked 'Where are you going?' or 'When will you be back?'" she says. "I got the message: You are safe with your horse."

OTHER PLACES TO SEE CARRIAGES

The Wethersfield Carriage Collection
214 Pugsley Hill Road
Amenia, New York 12501

The Winmill Collection
Morven Park
The Westmoreland Davis Memorial Foundation, Inc.
Leesburg, Virginia 20178

OPPOSITE, CLOCKWISE FROM TOP LEFT: All materials used in restoring the carriages and the coachman's livery are identical to the original. Four white faux Kladruby horses and a coachman's state uniform for the 1850 Armbruster Golden Carriage Dress Chariot of Emperor Franz Josef I and Empress Elizabeth I of Austria are displayed at the Florida Carriage Museum and Resort. Formal livery of the guard who blows the horn. A tailgate from a bygone era. An expert wheelwright was consulted for the restoration of the state coach. Everything down to the silk upholstery, piping, and tassels is authentic; even the cushions were refilled with horsehair and sea grass. ABOVE: Gloria Austin.

FREQUENT FLYERS

It is shortly after eleven A.M. as a 727-200 cargo plane approaches the runway and lands at the Ontario, California, airport. Less than a dozen people are waiting to greet the passengers. The plane taxis into place on a remote corner of the tarmac, far from the passenger terminal. Its engines expel a high-pitched whistle as they shut down, and a member of the ground crew rolls a ramp into place.

An enormous door on the left side, in front of the wing, has been made especially for this plane. Gradually, it opens upward. One of the passengers turns his head and takes a deep breath. Then he lets out a loud neigh, which reverberates to the back of the plane. One of the other nineteen horses on board answers his call.

There is nothing frantic in their whinnies, because all of these horses are frequent flyers. Down the long red ramp they file in an orderly fashion. The ramp was designed by the late Tex Sutton, who started hauling horses through the friendly skies in 1969. The business that bears his name continues to transport 250 horses per month around the globe, including twenty-five Kentucky Derby winners, among them Secretariat, Seattle Slew, Barbaro, and Street Sense.

Horse trailers waiting near the jet are lined up according to the "seating" chart. That way, the horses systematically descend the ramp and step immediately onto a waiting truck. Everything proceeds like clockwork. Airport officials and customs agents check their papers and passports.

Passports?

Yes, that's right. A horse that competes and travels in international events must have a proper passport documenting vital statistics, color and markings, ownership, and veterinary information, particularly its up-to-date vaccinations. Equine passports cost $300 and must be renewed every four years.

The cost of equine aviation transport can exceed several thousand dollars for transcontinental and transatlantic flights. The plane's interior has been converted to hold horses. It has a special reinforced floor and individual stalls that were custom built for the airplane.

"Our stall configurations resemble the inside of a horse van," says Greg Otteson, who is a vice president of the company. "Horses can ride three abreast or two abreast, depending on the size of the horse. We have seven stall sections and seating for the human attendants in the back of the aircraft."

It's nothing but first class on this jet. If a horse gets a sudden case of acrophobia or aviatophobia, equine cocktails (tranquilizers administered by expert in-flight horsemen) are available.

"When the horses lean or shift, you can feel it," says pilot Dennis Lamecker, who happens to own Western horses at his home in Tulsa. He trains other pilots in the skills of flying high-priced four-legged cargo, such as determining the difference between the similar sounds of a horse kicking and an engine compressor stalling. Keeping the horses calm during takeoff and landing is especially important, according to Dennis, who has also flown exotic zoo animals such as tigers, lions, and bears. "It's all about being smooth," he says.

MEMBERS ONLY

Horse owners spare no expense when it comes to the care and pampering of their most prized equine possessions, and a wide variety of practitioners specializing in aerobic exercise and health, among other disciplines, have focused on a burgeoning horsey clientele.

Take a horse swimming pool, for example. Horses are natural swimmers. At the annual Chincoteague Volunteer Fire Company Pony Penning and Auction, held each July, a herd of about sixty small wild horses (fondly referred to as ponies) swims across Assateague Channel and are then put up for sale. Author Marguerite Henry and illustrator Wesley Dennis imprinted this event on the imagination of countless children with their endearing book *Misty of Chincoteague,* published in 1947.

Then there's the true story of a racehorse in Canada named Puss N Boots. The horse was leading the pack as it headed down the stretch in 1961. But instead of dashing straight for the finish line and a glorious victory, he made a sharp detour to swim in the infield lake and unseated his jockey, Ronnie Behrens. The Puss N Boots Turf Stakes is now held in his honor each summer at Fort Erie Racetrack near Ontario.

Aside from the recreational dip of Puss N Boots, swimming therapy is an ideal way to improve a horse's fitness, stamina, and general health.

Human runners often head to the local lap pool to continue working out when their feet, knees, hips, and backs become too sore to absorb the pounding of miles on the road or track, and the same principle applies to horses.

A pool reduces the chance of injury following the repetitive stress on joints, tendons, and bones inherent in galloping or working a horse on hard ground. Some owners and trainers choose hydrotherapy as a safe form of exercise and rehabilitation.

Racehorse owners Gretchen and Bill Devers operate the Lazy River Swim Club, Rehab & Training Center at their Great Oaks Farm in Upperville, Virginia. The members here are horses.

"They only have so many miles on their legs in a lifetime," Bill Devers says. "If you see a little swelling in the ankle one day, you can put them in the pool and keep them going. They get their heart rate up for aerobic exercise, too."

Ten minutes of swimming is equivalent to about one hour of work on dry land around a training track. With the flotation, further injury, along with wear and tear on fragile joints, is minimized. The Deverses' equine pool measures 54 by 34 feet, with a 10-foot depth and a 30-foot entrance ramp. There is a 2-foot cantilevered deck all around so the horse's hooves do not hit the side of the heated pool. Four pumps in the custom-made pool can create a current up to 5 miles per hour to increase the tempo of the swim.

"When the horses get in, they really have to swim. There's no touching the ground," Devers says. An attendant walking on the deck and holding a rope leads the horses down the slope and guides them around the pool. "They cannot misbehave in the water as much as they can on land," he adds, to emphasize how a temperamental

<207>

Thoroughbred might spook at something as trivial as a piece of paper in its line of sight and then take a bad step on a training track and twist a joint or tear a ligament. "Every time a horse gallops, something can happen."

The pool is not just for rehabilitation; many trainers use it as a regular part of their conditioning program. The membership fee at the Lazy River Swim Club is $500 a year, and each half-hour session is $20. With an appointment time to take a dip, the horses do not have to wait for their turn to do laps. When they come out of the pool, they are hosed off and walked out until dry. On cool mornings, the horses might be covered with a full-length blanket or a fly sheet.

The Deverses train and groom their racehorses. Bill Devers got his trainer's license in 1981 and races his horses in Maryland, Virginia, West Virginia, and Florida. During the mid-1980s, his horse, Tutorial, set numerous records at the Charles Town racetrack in West Virginia. "He was my big horse," Devers says one afternoon after all the horses have been exercised in the pool. "He didn't win the Derby, but he was my big horse."

The Deverses also board others' horses for training and rehab. Gretchen grew up riding, and after college and a career as a risk management consultant, she settled down to life on the 86-acre farm. The Deverses and other horse lovers believe that nothing is too good when it comes to pampering their four-legged friends.

For horse owners of an indulgent mind such as these, Stacey Palmer Small of Pottstown, Pennsylvania, offers just the right herbal remedies through her business, Equilite. These include products such as GinZing, a blend of ginseng with herbs, and Equinacea, with echinacea for symptoms of a cold. Stacey also carries topical liniments, shampoos, and magnetic leg and body wraps—not to mention Equi Essences, which are flower essences in a bottle.

The Equilite catalog description for the Clear Thinking remedy pitches a product that "helps animals that are spaced out, unfocused, easily distracted, and overwhelmed by external stimuli." Another called Ego Builder "helps those animals that experience a lack of self-confidence and are afraid to face new situations."

When it comes to a favorite horse, an owner will do whatever it takes to keep things happy down in the barn.

OPPOSITE, ABOVE: Some horses exercise on a treadmill. TOP: Braiding the manes takes several hours of intricate work. ABOVE: Daily exercise for some horses includes swimming, followed by a bath and maybe even an equine manicure.

AN ENTERTAINING PRODUCTION

Virginia Fout often has to wind her way through midafternoon traffic along Wiltshire Boulevard in Los Angeles when she heads home after riding her horse. Brookway Stables at Middle Ranch near Hansen Dam and the National Forest is a relatively uncomplicated thirty-minute drive each way.

This commercial section of Wiltshire, known as the Miracle Mile, between Fairfax and LaBrea Avenues, includes many retail establishments housed in tall Art Deco buildings. The area was developed in the 1920s and is noted in the history of modern urban planning for its then inventive orientation to the automobile.

Virginia lives on a quiet street off the Miracle Mile in a two-story 1927 Spanish Tudor home she shares with her husband, Mike Whetstone, as well as Tiggy, a bouncy Jack Russell terrier, and Zoe, a yellow Labrador retriever. "We joke and call Zoe the Welcome Wagon because she loves to greet everyone," Virginia says.

Behind the black iron front gate that opens to a grand redbrick front courtyard, the inside of the house offers a hint of a life intertwined with the entertainment business. A pair of colossal stage lights temporarily sits beside a pot filled with red geraniums. An oversize outdoor dining table and several chaises longues are the perfect complements for their occasional alfresco parties.

Virginia is a transplanted horse lover from The Plains, Virginia, and the owner of V Productions, an event company with celebrity clients that include Elton John. She also has deep family roots in the wide-open spaces of the Great Commonwealth. Her late father, Paul Fout, trained

steeplechase horses, including the 1975 champion, Life's Illusion, owned by Virginia Guest.

Riding clearly runs in the family. Virginia's brother, Doug Fout (featured in "Trick or Treat," page 44), has followed in his father's footsteps as a trainer, and her sister, Nina, won a bronze medal in equestrian competition for the United States team at the 2000 Olympics in Sydney, Australia.

Virginia and Mike purchased the 3,800-square-foot home in 2004, and their respective backgrounds—equine and entertainment—are reflected in its décor. "We were one of only three couples who came to see it by appointment only," she says. "It was at the height of the buying frenzy, and things were going way over asking. We were lucky because it was a place of business for the owner. He didn't want the typical Sunday open house. We had to look at it fast. When you entered, you had to visualize the potential."

That was no problem for Mike, a production designer for television, commercials, music videos, and film. He has just come home from wrapping the final episode of Larry David's HBO comedy *Curb Your Enthusiasm*.

"I fell in love with the house the minute I walked in the door," Virginia adds, even though it had been used as an office. The entire place was carpeted, the foyer had a receptionist desk, and the living room had been broken up into four cubicles, with a corner occupied by a copying machine. The dining room had served as a conference room, and each of the five bedrooms was being used as an office.

"The kitchen didn't have one appliance in it, except for a

microwave on the counter and a small fridge for the staff's lunch," Mike adds. Still, the couple saw great possibilities, and the purchase was completed in a whirlwind three days.

Virginia and Mike were able to draw on their work experiences while renovating. His career in production design has given him a BlackBerry full of contact information for carpenters and contractors he uses for his jobs, where he is constantly creating new faux environments. Virginia's eye for detail, honed by putting together parties and sit-down dinners for as many as six hundred guests, was also invaluable in the renovation process.

On the night they closed on the purchase, they pulled out a crowbar and began to rip up three layers of linoleum on the kitchen floor. "The style changes over the years were obvious going layer by layer. Finally, we hit wood," Virginia says. "That was it. We decided to pull up the linoleum and have wood floors in our kitchen. It was just one of many discoveries with this house."

The couple had been in the house for only four days when they returned from an errand to find eight fire trucks in front of their new treasure. Firemen were hacking through the roof with a chain saw. A plumber had been welding pipes under the house, which triggered a fire.

"It was like nothing I've ever experienced," Virginia says. "Luckily, the house didn't burn down."

Following three months of living in a hotel, they were able to move back home. They were listed as the general contractors and continued the restoration process at what she calls "warp speed"—a somewhat typical type A pace in this area of the country.

"We did three bathrooms, knocked out walls in the kitchen, repainted the entire house, pulled up the carpet, and redid the floors in just six weeks," Mike explains.

"The challenge of the space was really trying to keep some of the integrity of the history intact but still modernizing things," Virginia adds. "The great part is the

PREVIOUS PAGES: The entrance courtyard of Virginia Fout and Mike Whestone's Spanish Tudor home in Los Angeles. ABOVE: Virginia, Tiggy, and Zoe. LEFT: Virginia's late mother, Eve Prime Fout, did the miniature painting of a Jack Russell. OPPOSITE: The mahogany chest was a wedding gift from a group of friends. Virginia found the hunt print at a thrift shop on Santa Monica Boulevard.

HORSES IN HOLLYWOOD

Beyond the silver screen, horses have been a part of the Hollywood lifestyle for many years. Actor Tab Hunter, now in his late seventies, once said, "Horses have been my whole life." He actually changed his last name from Gelien to Hunter because he loved riding hunters and thought his adopted surname would look better on a movie marquee.

In Beverly Hills, horse lovers once were able to trot their steeds right down the middle of Rodeo Drive. The bridle path, now a flower-filled medium, was designed by landscape architect Wilbur Cook, and opened on January 10, 1925, with a parade followed by a horse show in front of the Beverly Hills Hotel. During the 1940s, Hernando Courtright, the owner of the hotel, named the hotel's bar the Polo Lounge after polo-playing regulars Will Rogers, Douglas Fairbanks, Spencer Tracy, and producer Darryl Zanuck. Rudolph Valentino, Leslie Howard, David Niven, Walt Disney, and Clark Gable were all polo enthusiasts.

In 1990, actors Patrick Duffy and William Shatner founded the Hollywood Charity Horse Show. It's held each spring to benefit children's charities such as Futures for Children and Ahead with Horses. *Hart to Hart* costar Robert Wagner has also hosted a celebrity polo event at the Los Angeles Equestrian Center.

The late Fred Astaire had a love affair with racehorses and with one of the sport's first female jockeys, Robyn Smith, whom he married despite a forty-five-year age difference. And a little-known fact about legendary director John Huston: He served as master of foxhounds for the Galway Blazers in Ireland. The horse tradition continues in Hollywood with adorable actress Dakota Fanning, who became smitten with riding while preparing for her role in the film *Dreamer*. After the triple-Kleenex tearjerker movie was completed, costar Kurt Russell gave her a palomino named Goldie, named for his longtime companion, actress Goldie Hawn.

house has a lot of space, so with space there were options. The kitchen was the most amazing part. The walls are tiled and so is the entire ceiling, which is something out of the ordinary."

The original white brick tile was intact, and the room now exudes the feel of the Arts and Crafts movement—popularized in Great Britain by the designer William Morris—with accent tiles in apple green.

"We did everything we could to keep as much of the original detail as possible," she says, adding that they completed the kitchen by knocking out the wall to a former pantry and opening up the space. The hardwood floor they initially exposed with the crowbar now shines, but Virginia knows that owning a home "is always a work in progress to a certain extent."

Next, they tackled the decorating and bringing together of two distinct styles. Mike's taste leans toward the modern, and he brought a few living room pieces and miscellaneous chairs to their new home. Virginia

contributed a fondness for family heirlooms in the form of several fine pieces of antique furniture and a smattering of equine art, as well as a small and much cherished Jack Russell dog painting by her late mother, Eve Prime Fout, an artist and horsewoman.

Virginia Fout obviously inherited her talented mother's passion for horses. "I could ride before I could walk," Virginia says. She attributes her fearless sense of adventure to that experience, which later played into her decision to accept a job riding horses in San Francisco at the age of nineteen. "I was torn with what to do, being that it was so far away, and someone said, 'I bet you won't do it.' That was all I needed to hear."

While working with horses in the Bay Area, Virginia finished college at the University of San Francisco and the Academy of Art College with a degree in advertising design. Her career path eventually brought her to Los Angeles, where she was recruited by E! Entertainment Television.

"Still feeling very adventurous, I decided, 'Why not?'" she

OPPOSITE, BELOW: Virginia Fout with fellow horse lover Tab Hunter. ABOVE: After Virginia moved to Hollywood, she realized, "it's not until you move away and go out on your own that you realize how important your home is and what it means to you."

says. From there she worked in television production at Sony and went on to do event planning all over the world for Universal's Interactive department. "Each of those jobs prepared me to start my own company."

In late 2004, V Productions, "a full-service event production company," was launched. As her own boss, Virginia found time to return to riding. She has a young horse her late father had been training as a racehorse and is schooling him over jumps and competing in horse shows.

"There's nothing like taking a young horse and watching him grow, especially when horses are in your blood," Virginia says. "When I come into the barn, he perks up and gives me a whinny. He loves peppermint treats and carrots."

No wonder there's also a touch of horse in their California home.

"With my background, I certainly have a few particular horsey items," she says. "But I'm not someone who has to have every picture or sit-about be a horse. The entire house blends our styles. I think it's a bit like marriage as a whole; you learn how to blend. We learned a lot about each other when we got this house. There were times I thought, 'What have I gotten myself into?' But like anything else, you figure it out, and the end result is definitely something that we're proud of."

Virginia and Mike began to collect art they both admired. "We've acquired the beginnings of a collection that seems to mesh well with the horsey side of things," he says.

A wood-paneled den has that old Virginia look, with a horse-head lamp and hunting prints all around. "It's not until you move away and go out on your own that you realize how important your home is and what it means to you," Virginia says.

Virginia calls a sweet small antique table the "spoon table." It once belonged to her grandmother, and she fondly recalls rearranging the silver spoons, which still remain inside, while visiting.

"Somehow it all manages to work together," Virginia says. "It's a learning curve, but it's something we enjoy together. There are always things you wish you could have done differently or better. But that's life, I think. Whatever we didn't do this time around, we'll do next time."

In Hollywood, they call it a sequel.

OPPOSITE: Eve Fout's bronze sculpture of a little girl leading her pony is now the Mo Dana Challenge Trophy at the Upperville Horse Show. LEFT AND BELOW: Each June, Virginia returns to the East Coast to ride in the Upperville Colt and Horse Show.

Part VI: Down the Road

IMAGINE NEW YORK CITY IN the late 1800s, with chestnuts roasting on an open fire, horses high-stepping down the streets, riders trotting to live music in an indoor arena at a private academy, and children cantering on ponies in Central Park. The clomping of hooves on the pavement may now be limited to mounted policemen, but the classic interior hardware, tack hooks, and bridle racks usually found in stables have been adapted for use in apartments across the nation.

Searching for these equestrian embellishments often leads to the Winter Equestrian Festival in Wellington, Florida, where specialty shops are set up for the winter season with an endless array of equine-related objects. Just up the turnpike in Ocala, some fortunate former racehorses and their caretakers get a second chance in the Sunshine State, and further on, an award-winning writer and his talented wife complete the new-old Kentucky home of their dreams.

At no time is an owner's love of a horse more discernible than when the horse goes all the way down the road for the final time.

OPPOSITE: Life with horses takes you on a journey, traveling to horse shows, races, and more. Many moments are filled with the gaiety of a Kentucky Derby party or dinner with friends. Down the road, some horses have a second career on the street, others are retired on a fancy farm, and some are taken in by special caregivers. In the end, they all hold a special place in our hearts.

<220>

UP THE STREET

Finding suitable housing for horses in New York City has always been a challenge. In the early 1900s there were more than 120,000 horses in the city—pulling milk wagons, collecting junk, racing to fires. In order for the wheels of commerce and service to roll down the streets, utilitarian stables were established.

The stabling for horses used for recreational purposes was more elaborate. One of the oldest riding schools in the city, Dickel's Riding Academy, first stood on the northeast corner of Fifth Avenue and Thirty-ninth Street. The Union League Club later built on this land, and in 1891 Dickel's moved to 124 West Fifty-sixth Street, near Sixth Avenue.

Other stables around this time included the private and exclusive Riding Club, a four-story brick structure that ran from Fifty-eighth to Fifty-ninth Street between Fifth and Madison. There were stalls for two hundred horses and a 100-by-105-foot arena. Members paid annual dues of $100; a similar membership today would likely translate into thousands of dollars.

The Central Park Stable was built in 1871 and designed by Jacob Wrey Mould, the chief architect of the Department of Public Parks. A combination of classic brownstone and brick on a base of granite makes up the Central Park Stable along the Eighty-sixth Street sunken transverse, in the example set by park designers Frederick Law Olmsted and Calvert Vaux. It stands as one of the city's fine examples of Victorian Gothic architecture. The mansard slate roof had low dormers and a hayloft, and a gable held a hay hook for pulling the hay to the second-floor loft.

The thirty horses kept there were used to maintain the park, with some even pulling grass mowers. One hundred years later, a staff of sixty employees with fifty-plus motorized mowers maintains the 843-acre urban oasis. It's all gas-fueled horsepower; no horses necessary.

Still, horses do remain on the city payroll these days, mostly used by the police department for crowd and occasional traffic control. In March 2007, a new 6,500-square-foot horse complex that includes a training ring, stables for twenty-eight horses, a hayloft, and an equine shower, all with a Hudson River view, was opened for the horses of Troop B on Thirty-seventh Street near Pier 76. The city has about a hundred horses housed in stables in Brooklyn, the Bronx, and Queens.

"To me, there is nothing more impressive than seeing officers on horseback," Police Commissioner Raymond W. Kelly said at the dedication ceremony for the new Pier 76 facility. "They add a sense of vigilance and order that is very important to the city."

The stables were equally important to the city more than a century ago. The Central Park Stable is not to be confused with the Central Park Riding Academy, located at Fifty-eighth Street and Seventh Avenue during the 1890s. The average cost of riding lessons at the turn of the twentieth century ran between $10 and $20, and a hack through the park went for about $8. Today, lessons from an instructor elsewhere start at $100 an hour, with a hack accompanied by a pro $80 for an hourlong ride. Back then, several stables offered evening instructions and even advertised live music in order to trot to tunes.

At Durland's Riding Academy, forty musicians serenaded

<223>

equestrians from the balcony every afternoon, and the gallery had seating for six hundred spectators. Durland's opened in 1883 near the Eighth Avenue entrance to the park on the Grand Circle, known today as Columbus Circle. It was relocated to Central Park West between Sixty-sixth and Sixty-seventh Streets in 1901. On the Central Park bridle path, Durland's horses could be identified by their distinctive checkered brow bands on the bridle.

Durland's ceased operation in 1927, and the building was sold to the New York Riding Club, which closed in 1936. It then became a public stable known as Aylward's, housing about sixty horses during the 1940s.

Over the ensuing decades, the number of horses seen in Central Park continued to dwindle. Aylward's closed and the building was purchased by the fledgling ABC television network in 1949. The original front was covered in pink stucco, and over the next fifty years, shows such as *Wide World of Sports* and *Soupy Sales* originated from the structure at 7 West Sixty-sixth Street. Studios and sets for *Good Morning America* and *20/20* were actually located in what was once the riding ring before they relocated to a sleek Times Square studio in 2000.

In Durland's heyday, its main competition came from Claremont Riding Academy, at 175 West Eighty-ninth Street, where the horses wore blue brow bands.

Claremont was built in 1892 by Edward Bedell, who owned several other stables in the neighborhood, including Cedarhurst, at 147 West Eighty-third Street. The five-story limestone, brick, and terra-cotta Romanesque Revival building was designed by architect Frank Rooke, who specialized in stables.

Claremont survived while other stables shut down during the Depression years of the 1930s, when many previous patrons found themselves no longer able to afford such leisure pursuits. Instead, some even spent their days on bread lines or selling apples on the street to survive the severe economic downturn. Still, Claremont made it through those hard times, and it became known as the oldest continuously operated stable in the city. In 1943, Irwin Novograd bought the property, eventually passing it on to his son, Paul Novograd. Many horse-crazy New Yorkers came to Claremont to ride, including Daryl Hannah, Andie MacDowell, Isabella Rossellini, and Jacqueline Kennedy Onassis, who had her horse delivered fully tacked up and ready to ride through the park just across the street from her Fifth Avenue apartment. Georgina Bloomberg, daughter of New York City mayor Michael Bloomberg, volunteered at Claremont as a therapeutic riding instructor in 2006. In May 2007, Paul Novograd made a financial decision that devastated Manhattan equestrians, closing the stables and sending the forty-five horses to greener pastures out of the city.

"And so we will never again walk along West Eighty-ninth Street and be overcome by the deeply nostalgic smell of horses, and may never again have the surprising pleasure of coming upon a horse and rider in the park," the *New York Times* editorialized the week Claremont closed. "We lose yet another world, hidden just up the wooden ramp through the high doors of the Academy. It was impossible to walk past it and not feel that it was a secret entrance to a different city."

ABOVE: The stables in Central Park. OPPOSITE, CLOCKWISE FROM TOP LEFT: Cornelius Curry, Edward DeSuling, and J. Edward Maher were members of the Blue Buds indoor polo team at the Central Park Riding Academy. Durland's Riding Academy. The game known as H-O-R-S-E (basketball), circa 1908. Equestrians could relax between rides in the club rooms at the New York Riding Club. Claremont Stables closed down in April, 2007. Horses and carriages traveled on dirt roads near Columbus Circle. At one time, there were stables of all sizes in New York City.

A GOAL
BASKET BALL, DURLAND'S

31

DURLAND RIDING ACADEMY

HENRY F. KILBURN ARCHITECT

1220 - 5 M

STABLE WARES

Gardy Bloemers learned to ride at an early age and went on to compete in hunter shows throughout the United States. After a career in finance that included stints in Germany and the United Kingdom, she was lured back to the horse country of Virginia. In 2003 she founded Gardy Bloemers—Fine Stable Wares, a collection of elegant home furnishings and apparel inspired by horses and equestrian sports.

Her collection combines the traditional beauty of antique stable wares with what also can be used in the barn and in the house. Gardy's strong international business background and aesthetic sense helped form her appreciation for the venture. "And I can finally get back to indulging my love for horses," she says. "After living, working, and competitively riding in Europe and the United States, I can also add an international feel to these accessories."

When not working in the showroom or filling orders, Gardy rides the dressage horses she keeps at home in Virginia. "Through my travels to all corners of the world, I've discovered many kinds of equestrian-inspired furnishings," she adds.

Gardy has visited some of the finest old and new stables in Europe, England, and the United States. She says certain elements essential to both horseman and horse have changed little during the last three hundred years. Stall sizes, for example, have not changed dramatically. Tack rooms continue to be a gathering spot in the stable. Stables do differ, however, in terms of the beauty of the actual structure and its contents.

The chandeliers in the Royal Mews in London and those in the Spanish Riding School in Vienna are exquisite. Nevertheless, a saddle rack is what it is, whether in Saumur or Wellington. However, since the late 1800s, when automobiles replaced the horse and carriage, the craftsmanship seen in some antique stable wares is not easy to find.

As more and more people use their barns as offices and guest accommodations and for relaxation, the separation between home, office, and barn is less apparent. As a result, Gardy's range of equine-inspired fittings is suitable for both stable and home. A good-looking tack hook becomes a place to hang a bridle in the barn or a heavy pot in the kitchen.

OPPOSITE, BOTTOM LEFT: When he is not putting new shoes on horses, blacksmith Joe Siton creates farm signs and other decorative objects in his workshop in The Plains, Virginia.

"As more and more people use their barn as offices and guest accommodation and for relaxation, the separation between home, office, and barn is less apparent."

ON THE ROAD

The lifestyle on the horse-show circuit is often a nomadic adventure. The season begins each winter in Wellington, Florida, with the Winter Equestrian Festival. Owners, riders, and trainers from around the world gather for eight weeks of competition for more than $4 million in prize money. Olympic individual gold medalist and three-time World Cup Champion Rodrigo Pessoa of Brazil and Nick Skelton and Michael Whitaker of Great Britain are among the equestrians setting up temporary digs for themselves and their talented mounts.

There are tack shops, gift shops, and knickknack shops on the show grounds. M. Douglas "Dougie" Mutch, an interior designer with a shop called Gracie Street Interior Design in nearby West Palm Beach, sets up a temporary booth at the horse-show grounds in a former blacksmith shop. She transforms the space with her signature Caribbean-Colonial style, using what she calls timeless motifs. "Monkeys, palm trees, seashells, coral—all are part of what you will see at Gracie Street," she says, "as well as orchids, sailing ships, of course horses thrown in wherever I can, and lots of tropical jungle animals."

Patrick J. Doherty introduced a new line of riding boots several years ago at Gracie Street's horse-show location. Patrick had spent several years on the circuit, working to finance his college and graduate school tuition as a groom and rider for trainer Don Stewart from Ocala.

After college, Patrick moved to New York City and went to work at ABC Television. In 2001, he was a par-

ticipating recipient of the Peabody, duPont, and Emmy awards for *ABC News*'s coverage of the 9/11 tragedy.

"After not working or riding in the horse-show world for nearly fifteen years, I made my return, but not to ride or buy and sell horses for a living, like many do," he says. "I had another plan."

Patrick arranged with one of the world's most famous shoe designers, Manolo Blahnik, to make paddock boots for the horse-show crowd. "It occurred to me that the equestrian crowd, comprising some of the most tapped-in fashionistas, would welcome a new footwear option," he says. He put his plan into motion through a friend who worked for Blahnik. "After a pitch meeting and many phone calls and e-mails pleading my case, the president of the company went for the idea. He gave the go-ahead to have Manolo design his interpretation of the paddock boot. When I saw the samples, they were better than I'd ever expected. I knew they'd be a hit, practical but with the Manolo sexy shoe personality."

Patrick's next step was to go to the Winter Equestrian Festival to introduce the boots. He did not need a great deal of space to display his samples, crafted in calfskin, patent leather, lizard, and animal-print leathers.

"The first couple of weeks were quite exciting," Patrick says. "A lot of people stopped by to view the boots, and many placed orders. I often heard 'Manolo boots for riding? They're too expensive to step in horse———.' I tried to remind people that horse manure was actually the

cleanest type of animal feces. And the alligator boot that retails for fifty-five hundred dollars? Well, alligators are used to getting wet and muddy; the boots are perfect for horse shows."

Singer Patti Scialfa was among his first customers. She bought a pair of the boots in chocolate brown calfskin for $995. Scialfa and her husband, rocker Bruce Springsteen, spend their winter weekends in Florida watching their daughter, Jessica, compete in the junior hunter classes. Jessica has won numerous blue ribbons on the horse-show circuit.

"From this point forward, I'll pick and choose the horse shows," Patrick reports. "The Manolo Paddock Boots will go where the show-jumping elite meet, like the World Cup in Las Vegas and the Hampton Classic in Long Island."

HORSE KEEPING

Equestrienne Sherry Robertson has traveled the horse-show circuit for more than thirty years and manages the string of show jumpers owned by Harry Gill.

Sherry's main concerns are with the horses, many of them champions. She says "organization is the key" when traveling with horses and setting up a temporary space for them. She always packs the same way: one trunk for horse clothes, blankets, coolers, rain sheets, and fly sheets, a second for tack—bridles, saddles, horses' boots, and all the leather equipment required for riding—and a third for saddle pads and equine first-aid necessities.

PREVIOUS PAGES, LEFT, ABOVE: From inside the temporary setup of Gracie Street interiors, shoppers can watch horses and riders pass. PREVIOUS PAGES, LEFT, BELOW: Meg Rhodes leads her horse out of the tented, landscaped stabling area at a horse show. The snaffle bit has provided inspiration for clothing, shoes, and accessories for many years. ABOVE: Manolo Blahnik paddock boots. RIGHT AND FOLLOWING PAGES: Equestrian style can be found at the shops and booths at horse shows from Florida to California.

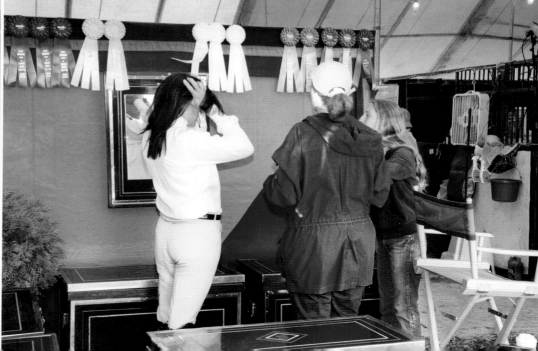

SETTING THE STAGE

Landscaping the horse show grounds is front and center of the Grand Prix jumping ring. Each show employs a professional course designer whose responsibility is to determine the size and types of jumps used in the Olympic-caliber events. The course designer also dictates the route around these high and colorful obstacles.

Once the jumps are set, a separate landscape crew fills in with brush, shrubbery, and flowers. Many of the jumps include the corporate logos of the event sponsors—Budweiser, Tiffany, and SeaWorld, among others—who put up from $50,000 to $100,000 and more each week in prize money.

Backstage, the owners and riders embellish their temporary space with flowers, stone work, plants, extra sod, and even outdoor lighting.

The result is a sophisticated patio feeling with accents of impatiens and the rich fuchsia and orange colors of bougainvillea (in Florida) or masses of geraniums during the summer (in Kentucky and Virginia). Some stable owners even rent plants from local garden centers because they don't want to take the plant material from show to show.

During the horse show circuit in Ocala, Florida, at the Horse Shows in the Sun, Jennifer Alfano, who rides and trains for Susan B. Schoellkopf's stables out of Buffalo, New York, is in charge of landscaping. She keeps it simple. "I use whatever flowers are available where we are traveling," she says.

One of the main jobs of the ground crew during the Uppervile Colt and Horse Show in early June is to water dozens of shrubs, hundreds of hanging baskets, and a hundred or so containers of geraniums, daisies, dianthus, lantana, and even more petunias and impatiens, plus several dozen ferns. "A crew of ten starts around noon the day before unloading and placing trees, shrubs, hostas, more geraniums, and other flowers, all color-coordinated with the jumps," says horse-show manager Tommy Lee Jones. "Each jump including the water jump as its own personal garden and often water jump has a waterfall near it." After the show, the shrubs are offered for sale and the flowers are given to volunteers.

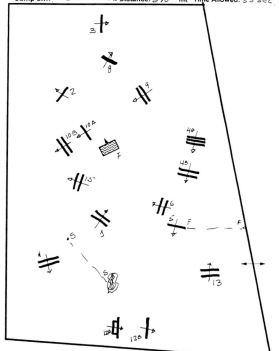

UPERVILLE COLT AND HORSE SHOW-1999

Salem Farm Jmper Ring 2   Date: July-13-1999

CLASS: 201 50.000$ Budweiser Uperville   Table: H.2.2(c)
Jumper Classic   Speed: 345 mt/mn

First Round : 1 to 13   Distance: 560 mt   Time Allowed: 90 sec.
Jump off: 1-5-6-15-3-RA-10B-11 Distance: 340 mt   Time Allowed: 55 sec.

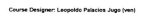

Course Designer: Leopoldo Palacios Jugo (ven)   Scala 1:600

Large dark blue canvas tack-room drapes trimmed in light blue (Harry Gill's stable colors) are used to decorate the stables. Tables and chairs are set up and wood chips are used for flooring in this area.

"You might say, 'Why blue?'" Sherry explains. "Harry says, 'If you show horses, your favorite color had better be blue,'" referring, of course, to the coveted first-place ribbon.

Sherry packs crates with everything from Absorbine liniment to zinc salve. There is an endless pile of brooms, pitchforks, muck baskets, and large (blue, of course) plastic storage containers. Each horse gets two water buckets and a feed tub.

Any piece of equipment that can be painted is finished in dark blue. "It gives the stable a stylish look and cuts down on theft," Sherry adds. All the blankets, halters, and buckets also are blue. Harry has a dark blue golf cart with his initials, HRG, on it.

"It makes it easier to find in a sea of green or white rental numbers," she says. "He even has the same blue trim on his car. We set up the stalls exactly the same at every show so the horses are familiar with the setup and take less time to feel at home."

Each groom has his own work area, with a bucket for brushes, a bandage box to keep the leg wraps worn by the horses, and a place to keep the protective boots the horses wear for exercise sessions and showing. There is also a horse vacuum cleaner and a wall box in which the riders can keep their own hat and paddock boots (Manolos, anyone?).

A large message board displays phone numbers of the vet and the farrier as well as riding and showing schedules. Each horse's daily exercise program is written on a special form. "The horses have breakfast at five a.m. and their dinner at three p.m.," Sherry says, "the same hours as when they're at home in Pennsylvania."

A hedge of ficus planted in gray boxes runs the length of one temporary barn. Pink and white impatiens in baskets decorate the front of a stable. Several photos of favorite horses hang in front of the tack room area, where ribbons on a banner flutter in the breeze.

From Florida, the horse-show troupe is on the road. They pull up stakes and head north. Some riders continue on to the Kentucky Spring Horse Shows, the Devon Horse Show and Country Fair in Pennsylvania, and the Upperville Colt and Horse Show in Virginia, founded in 1852 and the oldest horse show in the United States.

HORSESCAPES

Artist Steve Filarsky and his wife, Theresa Brown, of Franklinton, North Carolina, are among the vendors in Upperville. They have a shop in a 12-by-12-foot tent, and horse owners come by to look at their work or commission a painting. Theresa paints portraits of horses and riders. Steve does small plein air interpretations of the settings at horse shows and is frequently up early to capture the morning light.

While staying in Upperville, they live on the show grounds in a camper with as many creature comforts as possible: a portable barbecue grill, a mini satellite dish for television and Internet access, and folding chairs and tables to pull outside under the retractable awning.

"We get to the show earlier in the morning if we are staying in the camper," Steve says. "We get together with friends and have a cookout after the competition is over. And sometimes it's nice just to be able to leave the show and sit and drink a cup of coffee in air-conditioned comfort."

CLOCKWISE FROM LEFT TOP: Harry R. Gill chose blue for his stable colors because it's the same color as the many first-place ribbons his jumpers have won through the years. Steve captures the early-morning light in the main ring at the Upperville Colt and Horse Show. Artists Steve Filarsky and his wife, Theresa Brown, stay in a camper while traveling to the horse shows where they sell their work.

OFF THE STREET

More than thirty-five thousand Thoroughbreds are born in America each year, and as the meticulously bred colts and fillies romp in the springtime air, expectations are high for these future equine athletes. Still, for many of them, including some of horse racing's superstars, a bleak future awaits.

But the Thoroughbred Retirement Foundation has made major strides in saving the lives of aging horses long since retired from the racetrack. The problem has been particularly acute in Kentucky, the so-called horse capital of the world.

The Associated Press reported in March 2007 that the state "is being overrun with thousands of horses no one wants, some of them perfectly healthy, but many of them starving, broken-down nags. Other parts of the country are overwhelmed, too. The reason: growing opposition in the U.S. to the slaughter of horses for human consumption overseas."

Some equine stars are able to live out their lives in relative luxury. Consider the exquisite chestnut Genuine Risk, who captured the nation's attention in 1980 as the first filly in sixty-five years to win the Kentucky Derby. Following her Hall of Fame racing career, owners Diana and Bert Firestone brought "Genny" home to Newstead Farm in Upperville, Virginia, to be bred.

At the time of writing, Genuine Risk is the oldest living Kentucky Derby champion. Her groom, John "Buck" Moore, holds out a handful of tiny Tic-Tacs, and she licks one at a time. She spends her sweet days in the sunshine in the lap of luxury.

But the same cannot be said for another heralded Kentucky Derby winner. In 1986, a gleaming chestnut colt named Ferdinand won the Run for the Roses despite only two wins in his previous nine starts. His odds that memorable day were 17 to 1.

Ferdinand paid $35.40 for a $2 win bet as jockey Bill Shoemaker became the oldest jockey ever to win the race. For seventy-three-year-old trainer Charlie Whittingham, who had already been inducted into the Hall of Fame, the race was his first Derby win. There was joy in the winner's circle for owners Elizabeth and Howard Keck as the traditional blanket of roses was draped over Ferdinand.

Ferdinand was later sold to new owners in Japan for what was meant to be a successful second career as a stallion at a time when Japanese owners of Thoroughbreds were hoping to improve the breed. But Ferdinand did not produce as expected, and eventually his life ended in a slaughterhouse. CBS News did a report on his death titled "From Winner to Dinner," and horse lovers nationwide were outraged.

These days, most owners who sell their stallions and broodmares in the United States and abroad include a buy-back clause in any sales contract in order to ensure that their horses will never suffer Ferdinand's sad fate.

Still, horse owners and horse lovers are working overtime to solve the problem. The New York Owners and

<239>

Breeders' Association collects a voluntary reparation from owners known as the Ferdinand Fee. The money is sent to the rescue and retirement organizations of Thoroughbred Charities of America and the Bluegrass Charities.

Horse lovers Beverly Strauss and Ginny Suarez formed the Mid-Atlantic Horse Rescue in Chesapeake City, Maryland. The group rescues horses and offers them for adoption "as performance and pleasure horses."

THOROUGHBRED RETIREMENT FOUNDATION

In 1982, Monique S. Koehler founded the Thoroughbred Retirement Foundation (TRF) in order to "save Thoroughbred horses no longer able to compete on the racetrack from possible neglect, abuse, and slaughter."

The first rescue began with a nine-year-old horse named Promised Road, who ended his career with a sixth-place finish in a low-level $3,500 claiming race. Since then, the TRF has grown into a large horse-rescue organization, with many horses adopted by individuals who put them out to pasture on their own farms and care for them until the horses die of natural causes.

The TRF also has an extraordinary arrangement with correctional facilities in five states. The group designed an equine care and management vocational training program for inmates, with the state providing the labor and use of the land. Some rescued horses remain on the property for the rest of their lives; others are adopted by compassionate landowners. All of the horses make a significant impact on the inmates who care for them.

Janice Millard, serving a four-year sentence for pre-scription fraud at the Lowell Correctional Facility in Florida, was one of fifteen inmates involved in the first TRF program for women.

"I'll have a new career when I leave here," she says one morning as she leads Jimmy Jinx into the barn. The big brown gelding comes from the field with no lead rope. They walk together. As they approach the barn, she jogs. He follows in a trot.

Other inmates, clad in government-issue blue, are cleaning stalls and brushing horses. In a stall at the other end of the barn, Lynne Austin has a large syringe of antibiotic in her hand. Click Here has an open wound. "Go easy and check every five cc's for a return," Lynne says as Vada Ward inserts the needle into the jugular vein.

Lynne holds a master's degree in nursing from Florida State University. Convicted of first-degree grand theft, she has almost finished her nine-year sentence. "I'm a repeat offender," she says. "I stole over a hundred thousand dollars." Caring for the retirement horses, she says, "is the most incredible thing to happen in a prison in Florida."

In the afternoon, some of the women ride the horses that are being prepared for possible adoption. Just like their caretakers, they'll get a second chance, too.

When the women are released, they receive $100 and a bus ticket back home, but as one inmate involved in the program said, "I'm glad I came to prison. I've learned a lot about myself with my sentence. I'll have some self-esteem when I walk out that gate."

PREVIOUS PAGES, LEFT: Genuine Risk. OPPOSITE: The Thoroughbred Retirement Foundation offers rehabilitation for the horses and their caregivers.

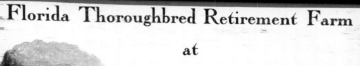

Florida Thoroughbred Retirement Farm
at
Marion Correctional
Institution
Lowell, Florida

DEPARTMENT OF CORRECTIONS · STATE OF FLORIDA

11021 N·West Gainesville Road

STATE PROPERTY
NO UNAUTHORIZED
PERSONS BEYOND
THIS POINT!

OUT THE PIKE

From the center of Lexington, Kentucky, the Paris Pike stretches northwest to Bourbon County and becomes Lexington Road. Directly over the county line sits Chez K, the 5,000-square-foot Federal-style brick home of Julia and Arnold Kirkpatrick.

It was inspired by the 1964 blueprints produced by the late architect William Wichman for a home he designed for the Kirkpatricks' friend Robert Wickliffe Preston Johnston. The Kirkpatricks wanted a home reminiscent of both of these men whom they admired, even if it did need to be updated. It has a time-honored front-to-back entry hall, which opens to a rear porch and pool area. The walls are paneled, with extra-deep baseboards.

"The style was the most natural of choices for this region of the bluegrass," says architect and project manager Tom Burke. "The roadway is one of the most scenic byways in the nation. The desire was to maintain and enhance the historic character of this corridor."

The house has "mixed antecedents," according to builder William Hurt, a retired high school principal who works on one or two custom-built houses a year and also happens to be Julia's father. "It has a nice classical look."

"My father watched every nail being put into place," says Julia, a manager with the Hanson Brick Company, of the eighteen-month collaboration.

"We used a lot of bricks," says William. "They are all set in a modified Flemish bond of a whole and then a half-brick every six runs."

The architect intended for this pattern and the use of hand-molded brick jack arches to create the feeling of old-world craftsmanship. "This is how it was done a hundred years ago," William says. "We tried to be true to that style whenever possible."

While maintaining the architecture of its predecessors, the plan was modified to include a first-floor master wing, larger front and rear covered porches, a main staircase in the foyer, and an attached garage. All of these renovations were done while keeping sacred the focal points of the house, such as the four fireplaces and the locations of cased openings. Strong communication between rooms was emphasized.

The dining room's custom-built mantel was designed "with a pilaster on each side for support and an emphasis on a straight line," William says. Built-in bookcases flank the mantel to show off a treasured collection of Royal Crown Derby china. The cabinets were all based on those plates, including the salmon color inside.

Julia started her Royal Crown Derby collection with nine plates and continues to look for them in antiques shops around the country. While browsing in a boutique in Dania, Florida, she didn't find her plates, but she did discover her dining room chandelier.

"I was waiting to pick someone up at the airport in Fort Lauderdale," she recalls. "I saw the chandelier, but I didn't buy it. Then, when we started to build the house, I wanted to get it, but I didn't know the name of the shop."

Julia searched the Internet and found a list of Dania antique dealers. She recognized the name of the shop and on the first phone call was able to complete the purchase of her circa 1920s crystal chandelier. Still, the story

JULEPS

The Appalachian region of Kentucky is blessed with an abundance of corn, which led to the development of America's only native spirits. Variations on a recipe of corn mash and limestone water aged in charred oak barrels led to Kentucky bourbon.

Paradoxically, bourbon is no longer blended in Bourbon County, Kentucky, but it certainly flows freely in surrounding locales under the labels of Woodford Reserve, Wild Turkey, Four Roses, Buffalo Trace, and Maker's Mark. Arnold Kirkpatrick prefers to use Maker's Mark bourbon.

For those who want to be authentic:

GOOD OLD BOY JULEPS

 1 tablespoon fresh mint, chopped, plus more for
    garnish
¼ cup water
¼ cup sugar
    Ice, shaved or crushed
 4 ounces Kentucky bourbon
    Mint syrup

Begin by placing a silver julep cup in the freezer. (And make sure you handle it by the edges when removing it later.) Combine fresh mint in a small pan with water and sugar. Bring to a boil and cook until the sugar is dissolved. Set aside to cool for 1 hour. Fill the julep cups with crushed ice. (This is key; ice cubes will not do.) Add the bourbon and top off with the syrup. Garnish with additional mint. Serves 1.

doesn't end there. The treasured light fixture arrived broken, but a local repairman came to the rescue. The dazzling chandelier now illuminates many magnificent smaller dinner parties at Chez K. The Kirkpatricks' good friends, the legendary Lexington hostess Anita Madden and her husband, Preston Madden, are frequent guests.

"This room is my dream come true," Julia says.

Arnold, the president of Kirkpatrick and Company, an equine real estate and consulting firm, realized his own dreams in the kitchen and library. He started in the vast open kitchen with the cork tile flooring. "I liked the look, and it's easy on your feet," he says. "The floor wears well, and you can spill stuff on it," he adds.

After consulting with his father-in-law, the builder, Arnold ordered custom-made mahogany cabinets online from Crown Point, a New Hampshire–based manufacturer. "I sent them the floor plan, and we settled the details by e-mail," he says. The horse-racing tile mural over the sink, which duplicates one of Arnold's favorite paintings, provides a focal point.

A tavern table in the kitchen provides an informal congregation setting for friends. The Kirkpatricks are members of a Chaîne des Rôtisseurs gourmet society, and Arnold tells visitors, "They have a chapter in Paris; Paris, Kentucky, that is. I had a foot rail installed along the kitchen counter. It's the same height as a bar, so I'd feel right at home."

The library expresses years of "observation and accumulation of design ideas," Arnold says. "This is a combination of everything I love."

PREVIOUS PAGES, LEFT: The design of the Kirkpatricks' home on the Paris Pike lends itself to entertaining as one room flows into the next. ABOVE: The stamp of initials on the bottom of silver julep cups indicate who was president the year they were made. OPPOSITE, CLOCKWISE FROM TOP: The walls in the Kirkpatricks' formal sitting room were finished in yellow to match the yellow silk damask curtains. Lexington-based artist Adalin Wichman designed the bronze Eclipse Award, which Arnold Kirkpatrick won in 1983 for his story on Nashua's well-known groom, Clem. Actor William Shatner and Misdee Wrigley, a fourth-generation saddle-bred owner and member of the well known Chicago chewing-gum family, own artwork by Douwe Blumberg, who did this small bronze of a saddle.

An avowed bibliophile, Arnold filled the shelves with the complete works of Ernest Hemingway and rows of signed first editions by authors living and deceased. There are Thoroughbred bloodstock manuals and reviews of European racing, which, as a former editor and publisher of the *Thoroughbred Record,* he found essential reference tools.

The coffered ceilings, covered in leather, provide a quiet library ambiance. "It gives the room a detailed look," William says. The poplar wood was painted with a faux wood grain.

Pocket doors open to a formal sitting room. Yellow stripes painted on the walls match the yellow silk damask drapery. The Kirkpatricks' equestrian style is subtle. A small bronze of a saddle by horse-trainer-turned-artist Douwe Blumberg sits on a side table. The painting of a jockey in blue silks over the austere white mantel is by well-known equine artist Katherine Landikusic. An English Toby jug of a jockey's head sits off to one side.

Almost as an afterthought, on top of a desk is the graceful bronze Eclipse Award, which Arnold won in 1983 for his magazine story on the well-known groom Clem. The bronze was inspired by an eighteenth-century painting by British artist George Stubbs. Adalin Wichman (who was married to William Wichman) designed it. Adalin is a painter, illustrator, jewelry designer, and sculptor who lives in Lexington. Her work also can be seen in the National Museum of Racing in Saratoga and the collections of Queen Elizabeth II.

The Eclipse Award, sponsored by the National Turf Writers Association, National Thoroughbred Racing Association, and the *Daily Racing Form,* honors the Horse of the Year as well as members of the media for outstanding newspaper and magazine journalism. Winners are selected by a panel of judges representing all three organizations. The award is named for Eclipse, a legendary undefeated British racehorse born during a solar eclipse in 1764.

Another bronze the Kirkpatricks own sits in an equally inconspicuous place. This one depicts the great racehorse Nashua being led by his groom, Clem. This sculpture was created by sculptor Liza Todd Tivey, who also designed the larger version on Nashua's grave, located just out the pike at Spendthrift Farm.

BELOW: The six-over-six double-hung dining room windows add balance on each side of an eighteenth-century George III chest of drawers. The walls were finished in two shades of blue-gray combed over an ivory field followed by a lacquer glaze, which adds depth. Decorator Roger Kirkpatrick (no relation) used Scalamandré coral silk damask and silk tassel fringe for the window treatments. "The drapery has smocked tops lined with English bump cloth to give them volume and soft form," he says.

DOWN THE ROAD

"You always were a bad horse and I always loved you," he whispered, "and that was a great ride,
and now—" He rose abruptly and turned away as he realized himself alone in the soft twilight.
The horse was dead. Then he returned to the tense body, so strangely thin and wet, and removed saddle
and bridle. With these hung on his arm he took the sombre path through the pines for home.

—Esther Forbes, "Break-Neck Hill," *Great Horse Stories* (1946)

Dealing with the death of a favorite horse, a championship Thoroughbred, a prized hunter, or even a child's beloved pony is never easy. Perhaps it is the sheer size of the animal that makes the loss so large. Grieving owners mark the occasion in their own special way. Some horse owners have large memorial sculptures done, depicting the animal in a favorite pose; others choose a simple marker; and some do nothing at all.

Sculptor Liza Todd Tivey received a commission to do a memorial for the champion Nashua to be placed at Leslie Combs's Spendthrift Farm in Lexington. Combs had a mental picture of Nashua being led by his groom, Clem Brooks, the subject of Arnold Kirkpatrick's 1983 Eclipse Award–winning article in the *Thoroughbred Record*.

"The piece was made in 1982 as a memorial after Nashua had already died, so I was unable to see him in person," Liza recalls. "I did, however, meet Clem Brooks, Nashua's groom, on a few occasions, and it was a help to be able to talk to him."

Liza determined that the bay horse, who had won the Preakness and the Belmont in 1955, was cantankerous and difficult to handle on the racetrack when he ran for then-owner William Woodward Jr. The horse habitually disregarded the whip when a jockey used it and often sidestepped when photographers took his picture.

Nashua was purchased in 1955 by a group of owners led by Leslie Combs II for $1.25 million after his original owner was killed in a much-publicized shooting.

Nashua stood at stud until he was twenty-nine years old and died when he was thirty. In the half-life-size bronze Liza designed, Nashua is depicted walking with his groom and clearly on his best behavior. The figure was also cast in a limited edition of less than a hundred in a smaller version.

The daughter of Elizabeth Taylor and the late producer Michael Todd, Liza fell in love with horses while spending her childhood riding in England and Switzerland. She attended Hornsey College of Art in London and the Otis Institute in Los Angeles and began working as a sculptor in 1979.

In 1999, Liza was commissioned by the village of Gstaad to do a life-size bronze calf that stands in the town square. After the 9/11 terrorist attack on the World Trade Center, Liza created two life-size versions of a rescue dog in the rubble. Recognized as an exceptional equestrian sculptor, she works from her studios in Millbrook, New York. Her other notable private commissions include Northern Dancer, Seattle Slew, John Henry, and Secretariat.

The legendary Confederate general Stonewall Jackson commemorated his beloved horse from the Civil War, Little Sorrel, in a very different way. Little Sorrel lived to the ripe old horse age of thirty-six, and a taxidermist was called in when he died to preserve his remains. The horse was mounted and is still on display at the Virginia Military Institute in Lexington.

<248>

TUERTA
1970 — 1985

YOUR HOST
1947 — 1961
BY ALIBHAI
OUT OF BOUDOIR II

TWO OF WILL ROGERS' FAVORITE HORSES
ARE BURIED IN THIS PLOT

BOOTLEGGER	SOAPSUDS
A POLO PONY	A ROPING PONY
DIED 1949	DIED 1949
AGE 33 YEARS	AGE 32 YEARS

SECRETARIAT
1970 — 1989

CHIEF'S CROWN
1982 — 1997

DANZIG — SIX CROWNS

CHAMPION 2 YEAR OLD	1984
HOPEFUL S. G1	1984
COWDIN S. G1	1984
NORFOLK S. G1	1984
BREEDERS' CUP JUVENILE G1	1984
FLAMINGO S. G1	1985
BLUE GRASS S. G1	1985
TRAVERS S. G1	1985
MARLBORO CUP H. G1	1985

d. 2000
DOSDI

"Perhaps it is the sheer size of the animal that makes the loss so large."

A debate about the remains of equine television star Mister Ed (whose real name was Bamboo Harvester) raged in Oklahoma, where a developer once claimed the now-speechless animal was laid to rest. He wanted to build a subdivision and call it Ed Stone until word came from Hollywood that the horse's ashes had been scattered in Burbank.

Evelyn and Dick Pollard of Saratoga Springs, New York, had their racehorse, Saratoga County, cremated and his ashes put in a box resembling a small coffin. Evelyn also had an image of the horse tattooed on her left leg.

Racehorse trainer Michelle Sharp wanted to cremate one of her favorite runners, but she "didn't realize that they put other animals in there at the same time. So the ashes are all mixed up." Instead, she paid $1,000 for an individual cremation. A box for the remains, made by the Amish in Pennsylvania, now sits in the bedroom of her family home in West Virginia.

"She'll go with me when I get cremated," Michelle says, explaining that her own ashes will be mixed with her horse's in perpetuity. "She's the love of my life."

WRITER HALLIE MCEVOY'S EULOGY FOR LOST IN THE FOG

Lost in the Fog's legacy to racing is more than just eleven victories out of fourteen races. Racing lore will remember him as a horse with an oversize heart that carried him more on wings than hooves. He lived and died a champion despite the cancer that lay hidden in his body.

And now, Lost in the Fog is lost no more. Godspeed, Fog. Thank you for reminding all of us that racing is not just about money, auctions, breeding fees, and deals—it is about fans and their relationship to a true warrior and game horse. Godspeed, Fog, Godspeed.

Lost in the Fog, "the star horse from the little track by the bay," was cremated and buried at Golden Gate Fields racetrack.

PREVIOUS PAGES, LEFT: Liza Todd Tivey's memorial for Nashua.

FURTHER READING

Christensen, Jo Ippolito. *The Needlepoint Book: A Complete Update of the Classic Guide.* New York: Fireside, 1999.

Cormack, Malcolm. *Country Pursuits: British, American, and French Sporting Art from the Mellon Collections in the Virginia Museum of Fine Arts.* Charlottesville: University of Virginia Press, 2007.

Firth, William Powell. *John Leech: His Life and Work.* London: Richard Bentley & Son, 1891.

Haseltine, Herbert, Malcolm Cormack, and Virginia Museum of Fine Arts. *Champion Animals: Sculptures by Herbert Haseltine.* Richmond: Virginia Museum of Fine Arts, 1996.

Haskins, Steve. *Kelso: Thoroughbred Legends.* Lexington, Ky.: Eclipse Press, 2003.

Heller, Bill. *After the Finish Line: The Race to End Horse Slaughter in America.* Irvine, Calif.: BowTie Press, 2005.

Hoff, Syd. *The Horse in Harry's Room.* New York: HarperTrophy, 2002.

Horswell, Jane. *The Bronze Sculpture of "Les Animaliers."* Suffolk, U.K.: Antique Collectors' Club, 1971.

Johnson, Pat, and Walter D. Osborne. *A Horse Named Kelso.* New York: Funk & Wagnalls, 1970.

Marchman, Judy, and Tom Hall. *The Calumet Collection: A History of the Calumet Trophies.* Lexington, Ky.: Eclipse Press, 2002.

Myrone, Martin. *George Stubbs.* London: Tate, 2003.

Payne, Christopher. *Animals in Bronze.* Suffolk, U.K.: Antique Collectors' Club, 1986.

Peralta-Ramos, Lorian. *The Mastery of Munnings: Sir Alfred J. Munnings, 1878–1959.* Saratoga Springs, N.Y.: National Museum of Racing, 2000.

Spooner, Patricia, and Victoria Spooner. *All About Riding Side-Saddle.* North Pomfret, Vt.: J. A. Allen, 1999.

Williams, Don, and Louisa Jaggar. *Saving Stuff: How to Care for and Preserve Your Collectibles, Heirlooms, and Other Prized Possessions.* New York: Fireside, 2005.

<252>

RESOURCES

www.equestrianstyleonline.com

Cover

Brass Tack Doorknockers
PO Box 732
Charles Town, WV 25314-0793

Mona Botwick Photography
PO Box 1710
Middleburg, VA 20118
www.mona-pics.com

The Sport of Queens

Dagmar Cosby
10413 Silk Oak Drive
Vienna, VA 22182

Equicizer/Wooden Horse Corporation
819 Dublin Road
Norwalk, Ohio 44857
www.equicizer.com

Ann Hagerty
PO Box 65
Butler, MD 21023
www.annhagertyarchitect.com

Champagne and Chukkers

La Dolfina
Avenue Alvear 1315
Buenos Aires, Argentina
www.ladolfina.com

Adriano "Nano" Perez
3500 Fairlane Farms Road, Suite #6
West Palm Beach, FL 33414
www.polomallets.com

Polistas
12-13 Burlington Arcade
Piccadilly
Mayfair, London W1J 0PH
England
www.polistas.com

Polo Bookends
PO Box 122
Rectortown, VA 20140
www.equestrianstyleonline.com

Scarlet If Convenient

Gala Cloths by Dulany
12360 Owings Mills Boulevard
Reistertown, MD 21136
www.galacloths.com

Well Read

Hooper's Books and Art
1615 8th Street NW
Washington, DC 20001
www.hoopers.biz

Undercover Books
4062 Roberts Circle
Marshall, VA 20115
www.undercoverbooksonline.com

Trick or Treat

The Pyramyd Group
Charlie and Toni Gauthier
6298 Rock Hill Road
The Plains, VA 20198

Katy Spier
Pruny Original Ribbon Blankets
PO Box 1125
Middleburg, VA 20118

Matt van der Woude
7508 Amberview Lane
Warrenton, VA 20186

The Wolfs and Their Horses

Country Way
110 West Washington Street
Middleburg, VA 20118
www.countrywayflowers.com

Floyd T. DeWitt
Calle Moscou 28, 51
CP 08005 Barcelona
Spain
www.floyd-dewitt.com

Gotcha Covered

Tish Inman
1151 Lakewood Drive
Gallatin, TN 37066
www.igotchacovered.com

Jean Perin Interior Design

PO Box 1581
Middleburg, VA 20118

Elizabeth Guarisco Wolf
Guarisco Gallery
2828 Pennsylvania Avenue
Washington, DC 20007
www.guariscogallery.com

Wild Whinny Farm

Joseph Piccilli
Chase Gallery
129 Newbury Street
Boston, MA 02116
www.chasegallery.com

Well Built

CMW, Inc
400 East Vine Street, Suite 400
Lexington, KY 40507
www.cmwequine.com

A Stitch in Time

Rita's Needlepoint
150 East 79th Street
New York, NY 10021
www.ritasneedlepoint.com

Well Worn

Ouisha McKinney
Ouisha Custom Designs
3984 Terrace Woods Lane
Lexington, KY 40513
www.ouisha.com

Big Man on Campus

Vic Hood
Leatherwood, Inc.
4231 Old Hillsboro Road
Franklin, TN 37064
www.leatherwoodinc.com

Ben Page
1206 Seventeenth Avenue South
Nashville, TN 37212
benpageassociates.com

Shining Brightly

Don Williams
Smithsonian Institute Conservation
Institute
4210 Silver Hill Road
Suitland, MD 20746
www.si.edu/mci

Equine Artists

Christine Cancelli
253 Kent Road
Howell, NJ 07731
www.christinemcancelli.com

Chisholm Gallery
3 Factory Lane
PO Box 943
Pine Plains, NY 12567
www.chisholmgallery.com

Robert Clark
241 Coastal Hill Drive
Indian Harbour Beach, FL 32937
www.robertclark.us

Evelyn Cowles
4677 Catterton Road
Free Union, VA 22940
www.ecowlesart.com

Cross Gate Gallery
509 East Main Street
Lexington, KY 40508
www.crossgategallery.com

<253>

Moneigh Art Work
ReRun, Inc.
PO Box 113
Helmetta, NJ 08828
www.rerun.org

Kathi Peters
Cob Cottage Farm
186 Weymouth Road
Morrill, ME 04950
www.kathipeters.com

Susan Van Wagoner
PO Box 58
Middleburg, VA 20118
www.susanvanwagoner.com

Beverly Zimmer
Forge Hill Sculpture
42 Aiken Blvd.
Warrenville, SC 29851
www.forgehillsculpture.com

From Tweed to Tulle

Daniel Sigal Enamels
508 East Main Street, Apt. #302
Lexington, KY 40508
www.danielsigal.com

Ginny Howard Antique Jewelry
651 Johnston Road
Lexington, KY 40516

Horse Country
60 Alexandria Pike
Warrenton, VA 20186
www.horsecountrylife.com

Live It Jewelry Polo Bracelets
Sheri Mount
International Polo Club Retail Shop
3667 120th Avenue South
Wellington, FL 33414
www.internationalpoloclub.com

Mystique Jewelers
100 East Washington Street
Middleburg, VA 20117
www.mystiquejewelers.com

Silks and Satins

Joanne Mehl Painting
4703 S.E. 40th Avenue
Portland, OR 97202
www.joannemehl.com

Lawn Jockeys by Kevin Titter
ST Publishing, Inc.
364 Fair Hill Drive, Suite F
Elkton, MD 21021
www.st-publishing.com/store

Sarah Marr
Episode 39
419 Harborview Drive
Kemah, TX 77565
www.sarahmarr.com

Silks Unlimited
535 West 2nd Street
Lexington, KY 40508

Starbucks

Tom Frost
Frost Architecture
41 Long Alley
Saratoga Springs, NY 12866
www.frostarchitecture.com

Pas de Deux

Susan Rubin
Beyond the Barn
11496 Pierson Road C12
Wellington, FL 33414
www.beyondthebarn.com

'N Everglades

Hunter Boot Company
Edinburg Road
Dumfries
Scotland, DG1 1QA
www.hunterboots.com

Robert Redd
108 2nd Street NE
Charlottesville, VA 22902
www.robertredd.com

Smathers & Branson
5013 Scarsdale Road
Bethesda, MD 20816
www.smathersandbranson.com

Ladies Night

Sandra Massie Forbush
Foxhall Farm, Box 149
Flint Hill, VA 22627
www.sandraforbush.com

The Horse in Snowden's Room

Kathryn Ireland
1619 Stanford Street
Santa Monica, CA 90404
www.kathrynireland.com

John Robshaw
245 West 29th Street, #1501
New York, NY 10001
www.johnrobshaw.com

Victory Gallop Group
1745 North Hametown Road
PO Box 551
Bath, OH 44210
www.victorygallop.org

Concours d'Élégance

The Sporting Gallery
(Royal Doulton Coaching Plates)
PO Box 254
Middleburg, VA 20118
www.sportinggallery.com

Katie Whaley
PO Box 899
Sourtnen Pines, NC 28388
www.hatsbykatie.com

Up the Street

Gardy Bloemers
6486 Hillsboro Lane
Crozet, VA 22932
www.gardybloemers.com

Joe Sitton
5529 O Bannon Road
The Plains, VA 20198

On the Road

Patrick Doherty
273 Prospect Road
Monroe, NY 10950
www.equestrianchic.com

Stephen Filarsky
PO Box 337
Franklinton, NC 27525
www.sfilarsky.com

M. Douglas Mutch
Gracie Street Interior Design, Inc.
201 South Narcissus Avenue, Suite One
West Palm Beach, FL 33401
www.graciestreet.com

Out the Pike

Crown Point Cabinetry
462 River Road
Claremont, NH 03743
800-999-4994
www.crown-point.com

Douwe Blumberg
3175 Highway 467
DeMossville, KY 41033
www.douwebronze.com

Stewart Architecture
161 North Eagle Creek Drive, Suite 210
Lexington, KY 40509

Down the Road

Liza Todd Tivey
537 Old Kings Road
Hannacroix, NY 12087
www.lizatoddtivey.com

PHOTOGRAPH CREDITS

Photographs on page 13 (top left), 17 (top left), 20 (bottom left), 23, 25 (top), 26 (top left and bottom right, bottom center, bottom left, center left, and center), 27 (top left, top right, bottom right, and center), 28 (top), 29 (center and bottom), 30 (center), 31, 35 (bottom left), 49 (top left and top right), 50 (top left, center left, and center), 54 (top and bottom), 56 (top left), 59 (top left), 71 (top and bottom), 75, 76 (top), 77 (top and bottom), 83 (center left, center right), 86 (top left), 89 (top right, bottom left), 94 (center left), 101 (center), 105 (center left, bottom left, center right), 135 (top right and bottom right), 141, 151 (center right, bottom left, bottom right), 155 (top right, center right, bottom left, bottom right), 179 (bottom right), 189 (top left, center right), 192 (bottom), 193 (bottom), 196, 198 (bottom), 199, 200–201, 202 (center left, top right, bottom right), 203, 205 (bottom right), 214 (bottom), 221 (top right), 227 (bottom left, top right, bottom right), 232 (center left), 235, 237 (center), and 250 (top left, center left, bottom left, center) by Vicky Moon; on pages 27 (center right), 65 (top center), 86 (center), and 119 (top right, bottom left) courtesy of Keeneland Library-Cook; on pages 40 (top left, top right, center left, bottom right), 41 (top left), 42 (top), 43, 114 courtesy of the National Sporting Library; on pages 118 (top left, center right) and 119 (center left) courtesy of Keeneland Library-Meadors; on page 34 (center right) by Howard Allen Studio/Darlington; on pages 13 (center) and 17 (center left) by Douglas Lees; on page 29 (top) courtesy of Polistas; on page 35 (bottom right) copyright Susan Ruddick Bloom; on page 73 (center) by David Cronen; on page 82 (below) courtesy of the duPont family; on page 83 (top right) copyright the *Washington Post,* reprinted by permission of the D.C. Public Library; on page 94 (center right) courtesy of the Maloney Family; on pages 102–103 and 147 (right) courtesy of Joanne Mehl; on page 110 (top) courtesy of Robert Clark; on page 118 (center right) courtesy of Keeneland Library-Morgan; on page 119 (center right) courtesy of the Kentucky Horse Park; on page 126 cour-

tesy of Cross Gate Gallery/Andre Pater; on page 129 (bottom) courtesy of Susan Van Wagoner; on page 131 courtesy of Evelyn Cowles (top left), courtesy of Christine Cancelli (bottom), and by Janet Worne *Lexington Herald-Leader* (center); on pages 128, 130, 131, and 132–133 courtesy of Chisholm Gallery/Kathy Landman; on page 139 (top right) courtesy of Sheri Mount; on pages 144 (bottom) and 147 (left) courtesy of Keeneland; on page 145 copyright the Jockey Club; on page 151 (top right) copyright Tom Frost; on page 153 (center) courtesy of the George S. Bolster Collection of the Saratoga Springs History Museum; on page 163 by Diana De Rosa Photo (top left) and courtesy of Mark Murray Fine Paintings/Henry Koehler (bottom left); on page 168 (top left) courtesy of Phyllis Rosen; on pages 176–177 courtesy of the *Pink Sheet*; on page 179 by Sandra Forbush (top left) and courtesy of the Washington International Horse Show (center left); on page 183 (top left) courtesy of the Lopez Family; on page 193 (top right) by William S. Henry; on page 198 (top) by Leanne Brubaker/Florida Carriage Museum and Resort; on page 205 (center right) by Baby deSelliers; on pages 222 and 225 (third row left) from the Brooklyn Public Library—Brooklyn Collection; on page 224 from the Picture Collection, The Branch Libraries, The New York Public Library, Astor, Lenox, and Tilden Foundations; on page 225 from the Photography Collection, Miriam and Ira D. Wallach Division of Art, Prints, and Photographs, The New York Public Library, Astor, Lenox, and Tilden Foundations (top left), the Milstein Division of United States History, Local History & Genealogy, The New York Public Library, Astor, Lenox, and Tilden Foundations (center top, center right, second row left), the George Grantham Bain Collection, Library of Congress (top right), and courtesy of the NYC Municipal Archives (bottom right); on page 227 (top left, center left, center) courtesy of Gardy Bloemers; on page 231 (top left) courtesy of Patrick Doherty. All other photos by Mona Botwick. Photo research assistants: Victoria Ingenito and Courtney Hill.

INDEX

<255>